Shelf Life

E11 ▪ E4 ▪ E18

Mike Edwards

SHELF LIFE – E11 ▪ E4 ▪ E18.

By Mike Edwards

FOREWORD

In 2008, inspired by my City Lit. photography tutor, Jose Navarro, I pursued the genre of Environmental Portraiture by taking photos of shopkeepers in my local High Streets of Wanstead, Chingford, and Woodford (E11, E4 and E18).

Over the next year or so, I gathered more images of local tradespeople, and had to decide what to do with them. I was getting to know the people while they were posing for me, and an idea formed. Gravitating towards those who had been plying their trade or vocation for many years I realised that there were so many interesting stories to be told. A record had to be made of their experiences.

It has taken five years to gather together 41 willing subjects, but along the way, I've discovered so much about the history of this area, through the fascinating stories of their lives which are recorded here in the first person. Some think they have nothing of interest to say, but I never found that to be the case. Some have come from unprivileged backgrounds, and have made a good life for themselves. Others have led intriguing lives and made the most of opportunities which have come their way.

But without fail, I have found a modesty and a pride in the work they have undertaken during their lives. Several are coming close to retirement, and since I started this project, several have retired, and sadly, one person has died, but I have included all these people as a tribute to their lives.

So, this book is a celebration of those local people who have dedicated a large part of their lives to their trade, vocation, or voluntary work, invariably with passion and commitment.

THANKS

Thanks go to my inspirational tutors, Jose Navarro who pushed me kicking and screaming into portraiture, and Geoff Wilkinson who gave me further encouragement along the way! My partner Kathy Taylor, for her well founded constructive advice, and her patience and understanding when that advice wasn't always welcomed. To both of my artistic, creative sons Ben and Doran, for their valuable input. And finally to all the subjects who selflessly gave me their time and good humour, for which, of course, I am extremely grateful. Obviously, this book would not have been possible without them!

DEDICATION

This book is dedicated to my late uncle, Derek Mead, with whom I wish I had shared our love of photography.

PRODUCTION

This is is a book about local people, and celebrating local business. I have therefore chosen to employ a local printing Company, Bindmans Creative Group, Unit 29, Bow Enterprise Park, Bow, E3 3QY. Tel: 0207 251 6006. They have used a high quality, environmentally sound, lithographic process to create this limited edition. I hope you appreciate the ethics of this decision, and the quality of their work.

PUBLISHERS

Published by Mike Edwards

E11

Wanstead

NOEL McMAHON, WANSTEAD.

LANDLORD OF 'THE NIGHTINGALE' SINCE 1987.

The abiding memory of my youth was being able to enjoy the freedom of the beautiful outdoors in Co. Clare where I was raised by my grandparents. I'd been born in London during the war, and partly for safety reasons, when I was just a babe in arms, my parents took me and my sister over to Ireland. I loved my grandparents so much, that when my parents visited us over the next few years, I felt scared that they would take me back to London again!

And indeed they did, and for three years, I endured the taunts of kids at school in London, purely because of my accent. Us twenty or so Irish boys had to stick together for our own safety. It was horrible, so at twelve years old I snapped at the chance to go back to Co. Clare! Although the Christian Brothers School I attended was tough, and the Brothers would be arrested these days for the forms of corporal punishment they used, I was back with the outdoors I loved. This time we got up to all kinds of skullduggery. There was a river flowing through land belonging to a big hotel, and we would poach salmon and trout from their river, then have the cheek to sell them to the hotel! Amazingly, we never got caught!

But by the time I left school at sixteen, I was ready to return to London and there I spent nine months in a basement of Woolworths baling cardboard. I then worked for the Rank Organisation, eventually supervising the night shift in the dark rooms, developing and printing the films. A move to Agfa followed, and later I joined the Post Office where I worked for ten years. I had a great social life and me and my mates regularly used to go to the famous Priory Tavern in Kilburn.

One night there I saw an advert for a job with the Chef and Brewer chain, so I applied, and there followed two years of extensive training. I was in my thirties by now and I had a year working on the relief circuit in West London, covering for publicans' holidays. My first 'full time' pub was the Black Dog in Twickenham, then followed three very successful years at the Waggon and Horses in Forest Gate.The next move was to the British Queen in New Wanstead where I spent a very happy and successful ten years, until in 1987 the opportunity came up to manage The Nightingale. That was the first time I had had the chance to be the landlord of my own pub.

This place has such an interesting history. At the front, Nightingale Green covers a 17th Century Great Plague burial pit, and later, for years there was a regular market held there. In the eighteenth century, the immediate area was known as Mob's Hole. Now, a 'mob' is slang for a pickpocket, or a ne'er do well, and could include the highwaymen who used to work the main London road through Epping Forest. There was an establishment here known at the time as a 'roadhouse', or 'pleasure garden' which was run by the self styled Lady Butterfield, who used to advertise her parties in the London Post, tempting the mobs and other rakes to attend. She was a Madam, which was hardly the behaviour of a Lady!! The wording of her advert is painted on the side of the pub.

Then the area was cleaned up, and this mid 19th Century building is now Grade II listed. Ever since I've been here, because of my love of the outdoors, flowers and colour, I've adorned the pub with hanging baskets, and every year I enter the Redbridge in Bloom competition. I won a string of seconds and thirds, until my breakthrough came a couple of years ago with a First!

This is a real traditional 'local' serving the community. We have all sorts of local groups, like the Rotarians, Friends of the Earth, Allotment Groups, Book Clubs and Green Drinks, using what we still call the No-smoking room for their regular meetings. We have live Irish music weekly, with up to twelve musicians sitting in, coming from as far away as Heathrow. It's very busy nowadays and although the job of Landlord is hard, I hope it will continue to thrive, as my youngest is only four years old! I had always wanted a large family, and I am lucky enough to have six wonderful kids who make up my own McMahon clan! The oldest is in his late forties. Lucy, my wife of many years, who I met locally, has gradually pulled me into shape and has given me a happy and stable relationship.

But let's finish with a story. The change in licensing laws ended the need for 'lock-ins', which were fine with the Law, provided you were quiet. But there was one memorable occasion some fifteen years ago when I was holding a wake for my just departed mother, combined with my birthday. It was a private party, packed with friends including many police, when at midnight an Environmental Health Officer knocked, and tried to close us down. Someone threatened him, so I stuck him in the corner for his own safety and carried on with the party. He got out, so we thought we'd have a laugh by getting the police to stop and breathalyse him. (Of course, it was negative). He got his own back when an hour later, the night duty sergeant came in with a report that we had kidnapped and held a man against his will! The sergeant and I have met since then, and fortunately he saw the funny side of it!

HARVEYS THE GREENGROCERS, WANSTEAD SINCE 1969.

PETE AND JIM, SHOPKEEPERS SINCE 1981.

Jim's story. **I first met Pete in 1980 when I went for an interview at the J.D. Harvey greengrocery shop in Highams Park. I was being a bit of a flash 20 year old, having picked up some redundancy money, and so turned up in a Jag. Pete took one look at me, looked all over my car, kicked the tyres, looked a bit menacing with his beard, and I think we took an instant dislike to each other. Pete's a few years older than me, and he had an old Escort van!!**

Before then, I'd come through a grammar school in North London where I enjoyed the sport, especially rugby, but I was a bit cheeky, and once got a burning red hot hand from a caning by the Geography teacher, who I'd just hit in the chest with a water bomb! Just desserts I suppose. I was very tall and strong for my age, so sometimes I got away with having a couple of beers after school with the rugby teacher!

I needed to earn money to help the family out so started working on cars, doing a job in the City, and had a part time job at a greengrocers. Then the advert came up at J.D.Harvey.

Pete was already a driver for them, taking produce to their shop in Wanstead, which later became the Antique Shop, and now the new Heads and Tails. (see page 27). Pete then managed that shop until 1987 when we moved to our present premises, which was when we started to work together properly. This was a greengrocers (JR Rowe) as far back as the 50's. I've been manager here since 1999, when Pete bought the Firm, but we keep the name as Harveys.

Fortunately, Pete and I get on much better these days. We have our differences obviously, and it's like we're a old married couple. Sometimes we are a bit bickery, but we get the job done well between us. We tend to keep our private lives to ourselves, but we have a good bit of banter. I've lived upstairs for 23 years now, so when it's my turn to go to Spitalfields Market, I just have to fall downstairs to get there at 5am. There's some really great old characters there, and no shortage of choice of veg and fruit with the dealers shouting their wares.

We aim to get the bulk of our stuff from UK sources, and buy enough to sell in one day, so that the majority of the fruit and veg here is very fresh, and ready to eat. As a result, we don't buy in bulk unlike the supermarkets, so our prices will vary. Sometimes more expensive, sometimes less. But a recent Channel 4 nationwide survey found that overall the greengrocers are better value than the supermarkets. We are also finding that people are getting fed up with the 'ripen at home' produce, which has less flavour and goodness than the veg and fruit which ripens naturally.

So we have a very loyal customer base, with whom we have a good chat and a laugh. It's always good to talk, especially with some of our older customers, whose conversations here might be the only ones for them that day. We also tease some of the customers, especially when they ask us if we are cold, and we tell them we have underfloor heating, which some believe and say they can feel it, too. But perhaps they are taking the mickey out of us!

One customer mistook our Aaron for a known singer, and kept trying to book him for their club, so he had to keep saying he had laryngitis, as she wouldn't be put off! He can't sing a note, except for West Ham's theme tune!

Some of the children who used to come in here with their parents years ago, have now grown up and are shopping here, as well as young families who are now moving into the area, as it seems more and more people appreciate fresh food. We'll be here for many more years I'm sure.

STEVE HAYDEN. WANSTEAD'S MILKMAN.

FLOATING SINCE 1978.

I might live in Tottenham, but I know Wanstead like the back of my hand, and I really like the people who I meet on my milk round in this district. Except maybe the Traffic Warden who put a ticket on the float when I was delivering to a shop, because it was unattended. I mean, how can I get to the doorstep to deliver if I don't get off the float? There's an S on the front (I think it's the manufacturer's initial), and he put it down as a Subaru!! They're seriously fast cars! Then one day, some Russians once referred to the milkfloat as a caravan! Takes all sorts I suppose.

They say you don't learn to be a milkman, you're born a milkman, but I had to wait until I was at school to help out on a round. Then at that age I could see myself being in the trade. I did enjoy school in Tottenham in the Sixties, but whereas most kids mess about in their early teens, I saved that until the 6th Form, so I came out of school with nothing. I'd also been doing a paper round and I worked in a shop for a while, but I think I was pining for the whine of the electric milk float!

I passed my driving test and applied for a job at the United Dairies Depot in Edmonton, and after about six weeks training there I was, on my own round at 19 years old, and I've never looked back (except when reversing obviously!) In those days, the float used to be loaded up for you, and the empties taken off at the end of the day, but now we do it all ourselves which makes the working day much longer. I was at the Edmonton Depot for ten years, then at a private dairy in Waltham Abbey for another ten, then back to Edmonton for a while, then here. Whenever I was new to a round, I always wore my Spurs cap, because that was a guaranteed way to get chatting. North London was pretty safe from that point of view, but I might think twice about wearing that cap if I had a round south of the River!!!

I've always liked chatting with people, and hearing their point of view – everyone has a point of view, and they are invariably different to each other, which is what makes people so interesting. It certainly makes my life better and I can put faces, names and characters to the orders I deliver to their doorsteps. I get the odd complaint about the time I deliver but I've got to start somewhere, and although I'd love to be everywhere early, of course, it's not possible.

On this particular round, I've got to know some people so well, that I've been invited to their housewarming and birthday parties, quiz nights, and I've even had the privilege of attending a funeral. I'd got to know this Arsenal fan and his family after I knocked on his door for his money when Arsenal were 2 – 0 up against my team, their great rivals, Tottenham, so you can imagine the banter. But when Spurs turned it round and won 3 – 2, I had to return and give him some banter back!!! It was all very good natured of course and since then, we'd all got on really well, so when he died of a heart attack, far too young, I was very honoured when his family asked me to attend his funeral.

The more you put in to this job, the more you get out. So you try and help out a bit. Some of my customers have my mobile number and one morning I got a text to look out for a dog. I spotted her and held on until the owners came and was given a bag of wine gums from the dog as a thankyou!! Whenever I find keys in the front door lock I pop them through the letter box, and when the milk is out on the step for more than a day or so I'll check up, especially if the person is elderly. On one such occasion the neighbour and I went in and the lady had been unable to get out of her chair for two days. We called the medics and they think we saved her life!

I've seen some right goings on of course and I get told who is doing what to who and all sorts, but my lips are sealed. I'm a bit of an Agony Aunt, especially to older customers who like a chat on the doorstep with stories of their life. It's definitely more than just delivering milk but I prefer it that way.

We deliver bags of compost, free range eggs, loo rolls, orange juice, bread, bottles of water, and the odd bottle of milk! You need a good memory for this – I have a quick look in my book before I start the round to check for any alterations, then it's off to 500 plus customers each day, and I realise I don't then look at my book once! Even if people leave a note out with the empties, invariably you know what's going to be on that note before you read it! It's mostly middle aged to quite elderly people we deliver to but things are changing, with some younger customers now as well.

Even though it spoils my social life I've always loved this job, but the winter is cold, especially this last one. My fingers stayed cold to the bone for three days at a time. Up at 2am, first delivery at 4.30, home by noon, quick kip at 6pm, then finally to bed at 9. It's always been a six day week, and, yes, it's hard work. But today it's lovely. Blue skies, nip in the air, blossom on the trees, my favourite time of year. Wouldn't swap it for the world!

CLIVE FENNER, WANSTEAD.

JAZZ DRUMMER SINCE 1973.

I was born in Writtle, went to the same village school as my parents and was taught by some of the same teachers. Maybe that village background later attracted me to Wanstead. I wanted to play drums from the age of eight and my parents bought me a snare drum and a pair of bongos and my Dad made a drum stand in the factory where he worked. I played along to the radio and started playing in bands when I was about fifteen.

First up was a 'blues-rock' trio and we did a lot of gigs supporting famous bands like Fleetwood Mac, Free and The Nice at venues like the Cliffs Pavilion in Southend. We were very lucky in those days as it was pre-disco and there was a lot of work. We liked to think we were like 'Cream' and we played interminably long solos until the audience walked out bored stiff or lost the will to live! But being in a band definitely attracted more female attention than football or fishing so I stuck at it. I had left school at sixteen and was working in a drawing office so being in a band was very exciting and opened up a whole new world.

When I was twenty one I packed in my job and went to college just because it sounded like a good idea. From there I scraped into Teacher Training College in Walsall and loved studying, so later went on to do a Masters in Philosophy, but at that time I had no intention of becoming a teacher. I met musicians at College and we formed a 'jazz-rock' band trying to play like Weather Report and the Mahavishnu Orchestra. We took ourselves very seriously, practicing four times a week and playing in the Universities and clubs around Birmingham. Those guys are all still some of my closest friends.

But I got married and moved to London to get on in the music scene. We came across Wanstead and loved it - it seemed like an oasis. Our first property was a flat in Hermon Hill and I've lived in Wanstead ever since. I went for auditions advertised in the Melody Maker and joined different bands, all of which were going to be the next big thing, toured in vans that broke down, slept on floors, made no money and in the end took a job and stopped playing altogether! For fifteen years I taught Philosophy of Education at Havering College. Yes, I was a teacher!

We had bought a house in the South of France and I sat in with the band at a jazz gig there and then played with them when they were short of a drummer. It was great and just what I was looking for! I took lessons from a very famous American drummer - Clifford Jarvis - who had been very active in the Civil Rights movement. We ended up good friends but he wasn't an easy man and he certainly wasn't going to give it away easily to this white middle-class guy. He gave me a hard time and really made me work but he was an inspiration.

Then, after leaving my job, home and everything, I started again as a full time musician, studied for ten years with Bob Armstrong and practiced for twenty hours a week. I attended the East London Jazz Project founded by Simon Purcell and Martin Hathaway, and through that met a lot of very good jazz musicians. I got some of us together and initially played in front of six alcoholics in a pub in Leyton, but went on to create a very good jazz gig that has been going for over ten years, and features many of the country's top players. As The East Side Jazz Club, we gained a following at the Heathcote Arms, then on to the Lord Rookwood in Leytonstone. We are currently at The Crown in Leytonstone High Road on Tuesday evenings.

I started a Jazz School in France which now runs for three weeks every August and then added a School for Cuban music every February in Havana. This gets me away for two months of the year, but I'm always happy to come back to Wanstead. Recently I got my own band together, The Clive Fenner Qt, with some very good musicians who I am very proud to play with. We have a new CD called 'Get It!' on Jazzizit Records. I am never going to be rich or famous or a great musician but I have loved the journey and I'm still improving and have new places to go. I have been very lucky to 'live the dream'.

ANDREWS BUILDERS MERCHANTS 1922 TO 2012, WANSTEAD.

BRIAN JOBBER. OWNER 1966 TO RETIREMENT IN 2009.

I've always been a local lad since I was born in South Woodford in 1944. My first memory is of relief that we didn't have to go down the bomb shelter, although it is possible it's just that I remember hearing my Mum telling me that later. My schooling was in Leyton, and I left at seventeen to join the Stock Exchange, because a friend was there. So, suited and booted, I commuted for four years, by which time I realised I was definitely NOT suited! I then spent a couple of years running a DIY shop in Colindale.

My dad was a builder, and he bought lots of goods from Andrews Builders Merchants in Woodbine Place in Wanstead. So, in 1966 he and the then owner were chatting and suddenly the business was his!! I started working there then with my brother, Derek, and unbelievably, I found some invoices which I had signed when I was seven, when my Dad had sent me in to collect goods for him!

Now lets go back a few years, to when I was fourteen, and I built a boat! We put it on a mooring on the Thames, and through this, my Dad inherited my love of boats. I sold my boat in 1969, and bought the freehold to the shop. I've seen the Deeds to the building, which was originally part of the Wanstead House Estate, being used as a barn, and a cowshed. The owners, the Wellesley family sold it off in 1884, and there were several businesses there over the years, until in 1922, it was bought by W.G. Andrews. He started the Builders Merchants, but he also made rustic furniture, and owned the woodyard at the back, which fronted on to Dark Alley, now Alley No. 122. There is now housing on the site of the woodyard.

My brother ran the woodyard, and an antique furniture business until the mid 80's, when he moved away. There has never been any sanitation or drains in this building, so I'd like to claim that I got the Council to build the Public Toilets opposite the shop by the bus stop! To be honest, I was just very lucky they were built there!

Over the years, I have supplied goods to big firms in London, local shops and residents, and Local Authorities, schools and churches. A huge variety of people have been through the shop. I know most of the other people of Wanstead who are in this book, and I even recognise the pot of paint stripper in Jim Godfrey's photo (p.17). I sold it to him! And I sold several 'Gent's back saws', like a small tenon saw, to David Woolley the denture man (p.25). I'm not sure what he needed them for, but they must have come in handy.

Being helpful, friendly, honest and enthusiastic, which were characteristics that came naturally to me, benefitted the business over the years. I think that my attitude must have helped people to trust me, as I was asked my opinion on DIY, and everything from Divorce Law and health issues, to making Wills and where to go on holiday! I smiled and tried to help but when queues built up I had to claim ignorance, so as to move them on gently! In the early days most customers were men, and they were more practical then, because in recent years half my business has been giving basic advice, like how to wire a plug or change a lightbulb.

I never minded going to work, but when I reached sixty five that was it, a veil was drawn and I could retire to enjoy more time at home with my wife, Jill. I watch her work in the garden, and I am also more involved with our boat in Norfolk. I do miss the people and the banter in the shop, but I won't be setting myself up as an Agony Uncle! I also miss the lack of stock or knowledge in chain DIY shops but of course that comes from being in the business for forty two years!

I worked out recently that during my time at Andrews, I journeyed there and back to my home in Epping 39,000 times. And I don't even like commuting! If I go towards Wanstead nowadays I start to feel claustrophobic, so it's the opposite direction these days for me and Jill.

Editor's note. In February 2012, the building was taken over by Geoffrey Rosenberg and renamed Stitch. Finally he has a shop where his family sell a wide range of good quality fabrics and knitting wool, whereas previously he, and before him, his parents took the goods to sell at various markets. And he has had toilet facilities installed!!

JIM GODFREY, ANTIQUE RESTORER SINCE 1980.

COTTAGE ANTIQUES, WANSTEAD HIGH STREET. PREMISES BUILT c.1780.

You could say I had my gap year very late, as it was just before I started working here. Long before then, having passed my 'A' levels, I joined the BBC and was posted to Bush House BBC World Service, where I qualified as a sound and telecommunications engineer. I was part of a team which worked a shift system to cover a 24 hour broadcasting schedule, being responsible for operating and maintaining fifty sound studios, editing suites, control room, Voice of America relay networks and other myriad technical equipment. And editing sound tapes, taking out a 'cough' or other inappropriate noises prior to broadcast, was fun in those days.

Then computers were introduced, the range of duties became severely diminished, and editing became less fun, so I left, and went travelling, taking my late gap year in the late '70's. Then the money ran out, and I needed to find a job, any job. Fortunately I met Ken and Peter who ran an Antique Furniture business, and they initially employed me as a general help, especially moving furniture around, and in particular, filling containers for shipment to the USA, which was a lucrative market in those days.

When pieces became scratched or damaged, I found I had a natural propensity for reparation, and so began my learning curve in my new career. Since then, I've developed many woodworking skills and established a large, mostly local client base. I really enjoy restoring a lovely old piece, and get great satisfaction from seeing the finished article, and the reaction from the client when it's returned to them, as it's normally a good quality, cherished item they entrusted to me. So the fun had come back in to making a living, but now from general cabinet making, marquetry, woodturning, carving, veneering, French Polishing and waxing, rather than computerised editing.

I also turned my hand to all matters associated to fitting out a piece of furniture, like metal working, soldering, and being a bit of a locksmith! But one strange job came in that was not associated to furniture at all, but required the use of the bandsaw. A guy I knew from a local frozen seafood firm asked me to cut some frozen lobsters in half. He was very happy with the extremely clean, smooth cuts, but a few days later, the workshop began to fill with the smell of rotten fish. The bits of shell and other waste from the lobsters had got caught up in the casing of the saw, and had thawed! A thorough cleaning was required!

My workshop is in a weatherboarded building, which is part of a pair of Grade II listed cottages in Wanstead High Street, built in about 1780. I think the workshop used to be a saddlery, because there is a set of very big brackets on the front wall, which would have held the saddles while they were being repaired, or finished and polished. Sadly, the lease on the cottages is expiring, so we will need to leave the premises behind.

I intend to take a second gap year so that I can build a new workshop and wood store at home to accommodate all the bits of wood I have never thrown away, and if all goes well, continue woodworking as a leisurely hobby. Furniture restoration is a very messy business, as it involves a lot of fine dust, dirt, stains and polishes, so I have pondered taking up gilding, thinking that this might herald a clean, bright and shiny future!!

TAFFY WILLIAMS, REAL NAME GERAINT. CARPENTER SINCE 1970.

ALDERSBROOK JOINERY, WANSTEAD, EST. 1963.

Why Taffy you may ask. Well when I applied for a job at Aldersbrook Joinery in 1989, Ted, the foreman at the time, couldn't pronounce my name, so he called me Taffy, and the name has stuck!

I came out of school in my home town of Harlech in 1969, and went to work for a firm of general builders. It may seem unusual nowadays, but they were also Funeral Directors. Actually that was quite common in those days in North Wales. As a carpenter, you would have thought that I might be making coffins, but they bought those in and I made the linings! I was also called on to help with laying out the bodies for the funerals! Not sure it was in my Job Description. Come to think of it, I don't seem to remember ever seeing a Job Description Form!

Anyways, after a six month Government training course, I worked with the firm in Barmouth until 1989. By then the work had dried up, so I decided to up sticks and come to London as I had family here already.

The first job I applied for was here at Aldersbrook Joinery, and they accepted me on the basis of my previous experience. So, having had my name changed for me, I got my head down, and have been here ever since, twenty three years and counting. In the early days, I did quite a lot of work out on site, including changing a lock at Buckingham Palace. I don't think the Queen was in, but mind you, I wasn't allowed to go and look for her!

We, that is, Aldersbrook, have done a lot of contracts for the part of the Government that looks after their buildings, so I have made windows and doors for their premises in London. I also did some joinery for the V&A Museum, but my favourite jobs are the ones which are one offs, like the gothic window frame in the picture, which I made for a timber framed farmhouse.

I used to make all the mortice and tenon, and dovetail joints by hand of course, but we have machines to do that for us these days. It is easier and more accurate, but I still have to set the machine up, with the correct settings and measurements, otherwise Ted the Foreman would have had a right go at me! Sadly Ted died last year, and we do miss his banter.

I don't have any plans to retire just yet, and the Firm is busy, so I think I will have to keep the name Taffy for a while longer!

FS UPHOLSTERY, WANSTEAD.

TED HEATH, UPHOLSTERER SINCE 1953.

MARLON LUKE, QUALIFIED UPHOLSTERER SINCE 1986.

Ted's story: **Yes, my name is Heath – Ted Heath, but there the similarity ends! For a start, I was born in Bow in 1938, and moved to Chadwell Heath when I was two years old at the start of the war. The other Ted was then apparently being elected President of the Oxford University Conservative Association, and went on a debating tour in America!!**

Straight out of school at fifteen years old, I was apprenticed to an upholstery firm, R.S. Stevens in Wood Street, Walthamstow. I was with them for thirty seven years until they went into administration in about 1990. I then worked two days a week in an upholstery firm in the heart of the East End, but I am now enjoying (almost) full time retirement.

I have always been an avid boxing fan, and I first saw a young local flyweight, Marlon Luke on the Channel 4 Henry Cooper Golden Belt series. Well, I recognised his talents, and sure enough he went on to represent England and turn professional.

One day at work, I saw the boss interviewing none other than my hero, Marlon!! I had to meet him, but was a bit worried that he might be like some other sports stars, with an inflated ego. On the contrary he wasn't, he was so down to earth and we chatted about boxing........

Marlon's story: **And that was what decided me to take that job!! I wasn't really planning to otherwise! Ted has always been such a lovely guy, and I regard him as a best friend. You see, I was boxing from the age of ten until I had to retire because of a hand injury at twenty eight. I was completely gutted, having boxed at all levels up to International, with quite a few trophies to my name. It was my passion, and my way of life.**

I had apprenticed in upholstery when I was sixteen, so after my injury and retirement, I went back into the trade to try to take my mind off boxing. Then, I met Ted at that interview, and he was the one who then, shall we say, helped me to reignite my interest in boxing. We have been to competitions together, and we talk about 'the game' endlessly. We never get bored with it.

I've been running my own business, F.S. Upholstery, here in Wanstead for thirteen years, and Ted comes in to help me out with tricky jobs, because we both like a challenge. There's been a few challenges over the ten years we've worked together, like how to move the studded, leather padded ten foot high wardrobes we'd made, in to a flat in Regent's Park without letting them touch a brand new carpet. We just about managed it! We also made a chaise longue....for a champion greyhound to sleep on!

Future plans? For me, Ted, I've got a lovely family and I'm happy with life, bobbling along, and much happier to have been an upholsterer, rather than a Conservative politician, I'm sure! And for me, Marlon, I am happy to carry on in this business, as long as I can spend time with Ted, and see a few more boxing matches together.

What's the punch bag in the workshop for? Well Ted hasn't annoyed me yet, but I want to keep on my toes, just in case!!

DAVID KEATING, JEWELLER SINCE 1968.

KEATING AND CO., WANSTEAD SINCE 1987.

At the time I didn't realise it, but my first seven years of life were rather austere. After I was born in '51, I lived in London Fields, sharing two rooms with my parents and grandparents. I slept on two armchairs pushed together, and we all shared one toilet with two other families in the house. So, when I was seven years old, we moved to relative luxury on the Kingsmead Estate. I had my own bedroom!

My first school was very religious, and I used to give out the bread and 'wine' at school services, and swing the chalice. My favourite part of school was my involvement in the choir. But then at Senior school any idea of religion left me. I was representing the school in the choir at the Covent Garden Opera House, with George Solti conducting, and while I was there, an incident at school meant that all pupils were punished as one, including me!!! I considered their idea of fair play to be different to mine. Anyway, then my voice broke, and went to pot, and the only singing I've done since then is on New Years Eve after a couple of drinks!

I enjoyed Woodwork and Technical Drawing, then left school at seventeen, and was looking at shopfitting as a career, but a friend of my Dad's gave me an opportunity and an apprenticeship in his shop in Hatton Garden. I took to it like a duck to water! The Technical Drawing came in handy with marking out designs, and after my five year apprenticeship ended in 1974, I stayed on and effectively became Workshop Manager. The company expanded, and my forte was in handmade jewellery. I made prototypes for the Argos lines, was teaching youngsters, and ordering the gold, etc. The whole nine yards!

So I decided I should do all that for myself and entered a partnership in Hatton Garden, which didn't last long, but, whilst there, designing and creating in the basement, my future wife, Elaine was working in the shop upstairs, apparently surreptitiously engineering our initial meeting!! She needed a partner to go to a Trade Fair, and told me I was going with her!! Once she had a say in what I should do, we decided to get out and set up our own shop.

Our first one from 1984 was in Chadwell Heath, which while a far cry from Hatton Garden, was fun and worked for us. On the opposite corner was the Tollgate pub, and the punters would roll in from there on their way home, to buy 'guilt' presents! Also, we did well with the betting shop customers, happily letting them spend their winnings!

In 1987 we moved into this shop in Wanstead, which had been a jewellers for the previous 40 years. I've always been happiest out the back, designing and creating, while out front I've got Elaine, who keeps the customers happy, and is a brilliant buyer. One of our daughters, Verity, is really into jewellery, studying hard beyond Level 4 and itching to get onto the bench!

When I'm at my bench, I see the shape of rings to come! The metal dictates to me, and the process is organic, not always ending up as I originally intended. I'll often melt work down if I'm not happy. But once, long ago when I was teaching, I smashed up one of my student's rings with a hammer because it was such a poor product – he was traumatised, as you can imagine, but we are friends to this day.

Last year, for the first time, one of my works was accepted into the National Association of Goldsmiths Design Awards, which made me happy, but I've now got the bit between my teeth to either win an award, or at least get a serious mention in dispatches in years to come.

With regard to this shop, 2012, of course, was our Silver anniversary, and at the moment, we don't have any plans to move elsewhere.

DAVID WOOLLEY, DENTAL TECHNICIAN, 1965 - 2009.

WANSTEAD LABORATORY, 1988 - 2009.

I reckon that while I was in this workshop, that's since 1988, we made up to fifteen sets of teeth a day, and despite slowing down a bit, that must be about 60 to 70,000 sets of teeth! Amongst those, I have dealt with a few well known mouths.

It was at the age of fourteen that I first took an interest in making teeth, so when I left school a year later, I was apprenticed to my uncle for five years, with one day a week doing a City and Guilds qualification at Borough Polytechnic in South London. I used to cycle there from Chingford to save a few pennies in fares. When I finished my apprenticeship, I did my National Service in the Dental Branch of the RAF.

Back in Civvy Street, I got a job with a dentist in Stoke Newington. He was a real character, and listed his other talents as magician, hypnotist and many others. He had a dental nurse, Pam, who I asked out on a date, and to my delight she accepted. We are still married after fifty years, and our daughter is a dental receptionist.

After working in several laboratories and dental practices for some years, I set up my own lab in this building. It was once a stables, but when I found it, it was an almost derelict storage area behind what was a Fish and Chip shop in the High Street.

The same technique for making dentures has been followed for decades, with only the materials changing. The dentures used to be Vulcanite, a baked rubber, but that was being phased out when I was starting, because of the scarcity of rubber during the Second World War. As a result, over the years, they tried using various materials, including a version of Bacolite, which was called Oralite. A wax pattern is made of dentures in wax for the patient to try, then this is encased in a plaster mould, the wax is boiled out and a plastic compound then pressed into the mould, and then hardened in boiling water.

No two mouths are identical so each denture can bring its challenges, and I do enjoy a challenge! However, as hard as I try to make the perfect denture, sometimes a patient just can't get on with something false in their mouth. I understand it's a bit like wearing a false limb! In the past I made gold, and porcelain crowns, but that's a specialist branch now. There's never a shortage of work, even during recessions, as the service is free to people on benefits. Mind you, when I started working, the NHS was brand new, and all dentures were free.

I've actually retired now. My colleague Malcolm had had enough, and I didn't want to replace him. I met him forty years ago, when he was a Teddy Boy. We worked together on and off all those years. We actually sounded so alike even my wife thought it was me on the phone when it was actually him! We still keep in touch and he still looks a bit like a Ted!

I'm carrying on part time in the laboratory that took my client base, and another technician, Patrick Fegan, has taken this old lab. But in addition, I'm a conservation volunteer with the Friends of Ainslie Wood and Larkswood, which is local to me in Chingford, digging, clearing and pruning the woodland. Also, I took my advanced driving test when I was sixty five, and I'm now on the committee of the local Institute of Advanced Motorists. I have the Family History group, and other local groups to attend, so how I found time to work, I do not know!

MASUD BEG, SHOP MANAGER.

'HEADS AND TAILS' PET SHOP, WANSTEAD. FIRST OPENED 1965.

I was born in Sailkot, Pakistan, and my Dad brought the family to the UK when I was ten. I couldn't speak a word of English, but boy did I learn quickly. I think that kids should be taught two or three languages in Junior school. Their brains are much more receptive at a young age.

Dad trained as a carpenter in the UK, but he never worked again after incurring a back injury in 1968. Those were very hard years. We were living in the East End on my Mum's income as a seamstress. She came home from work one day, to see all our furniture out on the street. Dad hadn't understood the lease on the property, so we were taken to a hostel. I was twelve and Mum, Dad and four of us children had to sleep in a big hall for two weeks. We then got moved to a house in Cable Street, where we were reunited with our two older siblings. That actually made it even tougher, because I remember it was a two bedroom house for two adults and six children!!

Dad somehow managed to get a mortgage, and we moved to a house in Upton Park, where we helped Mum work at home. She often worked at the sewing machine from 5am to 11pm, to earn enough to put all of my brothers and sisters through further education. I felt I ought to help her, rather than go to study, and eventually I trained as a mechanic, taking various jobs, and in the end, worked my way up to Transport Manager at Sunblest Bakeries.

There was a lot of pressure in that job, and I wanted a change anyway. So I bought this Pet Shop and Garden Centre as a going concern in 1998. We sell all pet supplies, small animals, fish and birds and some plants and garden needs. I feel sad when parents bring their children in to see the guinea pigs for example, and then refuse to buy one. There's usually tears and tantrums to follow. One mum bought guinea pigs and all the gear for £120, then brought them back five weeks later, as the children weren't looking after them!

One man brought in a couple of stick insects, which I bought from him, and which I'm pleased to say got sold in the same week. Then, my colleague Trevor had a couple of Giant African snails, which grow as big as the palm of your hand. They bred like fury, so we had lots of snails to sell. I recall a guy came in one day, and asked what they were and what they did. I told him they did absolutely nothing, and he said 'Oh good I'll have two of those!!'

I now stock far more hardware items since Woolworths closed, together with other bits and pieces my customers have specifically requested, like haberdashery. I think that was the reason I was given the Wanstead Shopkeeper of the Year award recently, but all I was doing was trying to help out our locals a bit.

The photo is of me in the old shop, but I've moved into the bigger premises next door just recently so have expanded my stock. I'll continue with the pets and pet supplies, and some plants out the front, but will have to forego the nursery I had at the back. I'm very happy here, having some lovely customers, and I hope the future will be bright.

EAMON EVERALL, ADULT EDUCATION ART TEACHER SINCE 1969.

WALTHAM FOREST AND REDBRIDGE, INCLUDING WANSTEAD.

I was born into an Army family in 1948, and spent my youth in Europe and the Far East. My early memories of Malaya during the 'emergency', were of being so scared at night under my mosquito net, that I used to pile up four teddy bears on my tummy, so when the terrorists came to stab me, the teddies would get it first! I was only five at the time!

I attended sixteen different schools over the next fifteen years, and as the permanent new boy, I got poked and prodded by the bullies, who I dealt with by saying my Daddy was a soldier and he would shoot them! I spent most of my young years with my Mum, as when we moved to a new place, the Dads went three months ahead to check it out.

We would go on holiday to Panang in the troop trains and I remember my Dad and the other soldiers firing rifles through the slit windows in the train at the local terrorists. But he was also a good amateur artist, and once we were back in England, he inspired me, so at the age of 18, I attended my local Folkestone School of Art. It wasn't a problem, as I had realised that there was a promising free spirited social life there and also I had been regarded as rather bohemian by my school, who were glad to see me leave.

Whilst I was an art student, aged twenty two I started teaching art to adults in Waltham Forest and then Redbridge, including here at Wanstead House. Adult Education has always been close to my heart, as I believe in education for all classes, which then brings out an added value for society as opposed to the 'herding' of mainstream education. Also it's good to give something back to society while at the same time I get a lot back from students, as they challenge me to look at the very concepts of art, and my own preconceptions.

Outside of teaching, I have enjoyed sculpting and I was commissioned by Waltham Forest to design a sculpture to celebrate the Millennium, which I call Millennium Temple, and which stands at the Bakers Arms crossroads in Leyton. I would have wanted it to have been even taller than it is, but the Council put on a height restriction. Then in 1999 I was a founding member of the Stuckist Art movement along with Billy Childish and ten others. The name Stuckist was a riposte to Billy's ex-partner, Tracey Emin, who referred to his art as 'stuck, stuck, stuck'! I am now, quite late, gaining recognition for my paintings through that movement, which is a 're-modernist, anti-conceptual' art group.

Since my mid-20's I have found invigoration and refreshment, not only for my art, but for all aspects of my life, through Buddhist meditation. It has in turn led me into attending church services again, of all denominations, where I find the communal celebration and shared joy of life very uplifting.

Where do I go from here? Well, with young children I'm staying put, which has helped me get involved in local community associations, both new and old. Perhaps my crowning glory is yet to come!

Why the cravat? It's certainly my trademark, but that's a story for another time and place.........

STEVENS MOTORS. WANSTEAD SINCE 1966.

BRAD STEVENS, OWNER.

I've been a local lad all my life, from birth at Wanstead Hospital in 1956, through school at the Nightingale, junior and senior, and into business life in the garage behind the Cuckfield pub. I've always enjoyed talking with people – in fact I remember lunchtimes at Junior School, continually being made to sit on my own, and being caned for the heinous crime of talking, which was banned by a particularly authoritarian Head Teacher! By the way, I thought the food was horrible!

I got 'O' levels in Technical Drawing and Engineering, which got me into work at Abbey Balustrades in Leytonstone, where we made – you've guessed it, balustrades! I enjoyed life there while we made railings for Horse Guards Parade, and a staircase for Jim Callaghan's house, but then my boss got a contract to fit out Brent Cross, which meant I was producing brackets by the hundred which became very boring.

My Granddad, Jack, used to repair Rolls Royce cars in Forest Gate around 1949, (and he raced at Brooklands), so motor engineering has been in our family for over 60 years. My Dad, John started Stevens Motors (initially in the building which was to become the Aldersbrook Library (p.33)) with his brother Cyril, who later built Maryland Autos in Stratford.

I've got two brothers, Brian and John. Brian joined his Uncle Cyril at Maryland straight from school, while John worked in a garage in New Jersey, USA, where he saw that VW Beetles were becoming very popular. On his return to the UK in 1966, he and Brian came together to take over the Stevens family business and started to work on VW's. They bought our present premises from Brian's father-in-law who had a car hire service here - hence the petrol pump. Before that it was a slaughterhouse, and some of the features remain to this day!

By 1976 I was disheartened with making brackets, so joined the business. We were buying broken Beetles, fixing them up, and selling them on. Then customers returned for parts and servicing. So we adapted and branched out to cover all VW models, and to this day, we do crash repairs as well as the mechanical side. We used to use sawdust from Aldersbrook Joinery (p.19) to soak up the oil on the floor, and sometimes we would lose John for a while in the cold winter mornings, then trace him to Andrews Builders, to find him drinking tea by the warm stove with Mr. Jobber! (p.15).

Our brother Brian would be the first to admit that his mechanical skills were better than his customer skills, and we moved him out of the Office, as he once told a customer to 'go elsewhere and don't return', because the customer had asked for a less than cost price on a completed job! Thank heavens he wasn't dealing with the customer who reported a rattle from under the car when he was cornering. After extensive road testing, we found a beer can under the seat! We didn't have the heart to charge him.

In the meantime I had met Lesley, whom I later married, and who initially told me not to expect to have children with her, as she came from a large family and had looked after her young siblings. I'm not sure what happened, but we now have three lovely grown up 'kids'. Lesley now works at Alan Days, the VW main dealer. We can't, or won't get away from VW's!!

By the mid 90's, both Brian and John were ready to retire, so I took over. The business is based on long standing and loyal customers, and it's only in the present financial climate, that I have needed to advertise, but I'm sure we will survive while we offer good value to our customers.

As for the future, I love this area, and see people move away, only to return. I know I'll be working at the garage behind the Cuckfield until the mortgage is paid off, and I'm sure I'll stay in the area long after that.

(Interviewed at the Nightingale pub, Wanstead – see page 7!!)

GILL JAMES. LOCAL CAMPAIGNER SINCE THE YEAR DOT.

LIBRARIAN, 1984 TO 2011, ALDERSBROOK LIBRARY, WANSTEAD.

I was born in Chelmsford at the end of the war. Much to my mother's chagrin, my Dad became a Jehovah's Witness, and took me doorstepping with him when I was eight. That was my first taste of campaigning. To get me away from that, Mum sent me to a Boarding School, run by Quakers. But when Dad found out it was a Quaker school, he tried to take me out, failed, and every weekend after that, took me to Witness meetings. My Sundays were two Witness and two Quaker meetings. I'm still not a convert to either!

After qualifying in North London to teach, I met Alan at the Highgate Harriers Running Club Christmas dance (he was the runner, not me). When we married we moved to Leyton, and one day Alan discovered the delights of Wanstead whilst running in Wanstead Park. We moved here with our two young daughters in 1978.

My Quaker schooling got me interested in pacifism, so I helped organise a local branch of CND in the 1980's. I'm still a big supporter of CND and the campaign against the Arms Trade, but I also wanted to do something that felt more positive in its actions and results. As a family, we were using our bikes more than a car, so I joined the London Cycling Campaign (LCC), and established the Redbridge branch in 1990. With help, I set up a cycle liaison group with the Council. It's still a struggle to get people to listen to cyclists' needs, despite its increase in popularity, but we still run cycle workshops at Wanstead House, and organise cycling trips for local people.

From that interest sprung the idea of re-enacting the Woodford Cycle Meet, last run in about 1912. We managed to get 150 cyclists dressed in Edwardian clothes to ride from Woodford to Wanstead Park, and had an Edwardian themed festival there. It was such fun, and so well supported, that I wanted to continue to get people together, and the idea of Music in the Park was born. The owners of the Park, City of London Corporation, weren't too sure to start with, but now, ten years on, they let us get on with it, as long as it doesn't turn into a Glastonbury! With the help of the Aldersbrook Families Association, (AFA) the event has grown into a £14,000 budget festival, attended by thousands each year.

While I was teaching part time, I started working at the Aldersbrook Library twenty nine years ago. When it was threatened with closure in 1990, a huge public furore was whipped up, and I got more involved than I should, but we kept it open, which was a very happy result.

In my early days there, I remember an old lady used to walk to the Library in the middle of the road, as though she still thought cars hadn't been invented. She always left with a cheery 'toodleloo". Another incident involved the booking of the only public computer in Redbridge which had been kindly donated to Aldersbrook Library. A gentleman from Europe was a frequent user and my colleague and I regularly calmed him if he couldn't get his 'slot'. One day we both were away, and a temp told him it was booked. The customer threatened to kill him, and with the police in attendance I was called to sort everything out! He was so upset he'd used such words. All ended peacefully thankfully.

I have many happy memories of my years there, and I retired earlier last year. Then, one of my colleagues, unknown to me, nominated me for an MBE for services to the Library and the local community. The first I heard of it was the arrival of the envelope inviting me to Buck House. Although it's not really my style, it is lovely to be recognised for <u>My</u> <u>Bloody</u> <u>Efforts</u>!

So, where to now. More holidays thankfully, in between the campaigns, tending our allotment and visiting our daughters in Germany. But I'm not leaving Aldersbrook: I love it, and the people and the Park, too much.

WANSTEAD PARK TEA HUT/CAFE.

JEAN MAESTRI, PROPRIETOR SINCE 1986.

In 1944 I was the last of three to be born at my parents' house on the Dagenham Council Estate where they lived for the rest of their lives, with Mum deciding she had had enough at 99 years and 4 months! She was as bright as a button to the very end.

My early memories are of playing on the bomb sites, and games of Rounders between four trees in the street, until I got called in for bed. When I came in from school on a washing day you couldn't see across the kitchen for steam, and as for bath times, well, the water would be heated in a big coal fired copper in the kitchen and there was a pump handle on the wall, which Mum would work to get the water up to the bathroom on the first floor. That was until about 1955 when the Council installed a geyser system!!

I went to the same school as Terry Venables the famous footballer, who was a year ahead of me. He was a nice boy. I left school at fifteen years old having worked really hard in the 'B' stream and I surprised everyone by getting a job as a Medical Receptionist at the London Hospital. 'B' streamers weren't supposed to look for work like that but I took a chance, asked for the job, and got it!!

I was there for eight years until I had my first baby. I had met my future husband Giovanni, in a crowded Trafalgar Square. I was only sixteen and this man behind me said "Has anyone seen my cat?" It turns out it was a chat up line, and I happily fell for it – and him, because we are still together fifty three years later. We call him John now and we have five children. All our names start with 'J'! He has put his hand to most things including making ice cream, and it was this skill that inspired us to rent the old boathouse and cafe here in the Park in 1986. It was in a right state and the cafe wasn't very hygienic, to say the least.

So a year later we applied to the owners of the Park, the Corporation of London, to get it rebuilt, and their architect designed the building to look like the Temple nearby. The boathouse went during that rebuild, but personally, I would love to see the boats back on this lake here.

I have been coming here doing the teas and cakes every weekend all year round, and weekdays from March to September. We even open on Boxing Day and New Year's Day, when it gets packed out with the dog walkers. We meet so many lovely people who come back year after year. I do miss the cows that used to roam free in the Park but I admit that it was a bit scary when twelve of them would come towards me when I was getting out of my car at the gate. I'd hop back in the car and wait for them to go away!!

I'm very lucky to have a family who will all help out here, or at least meet here, so I get to see them all regularly. And they never argue! I put it down to the fact that we used to foster children on a short term basis back in the late 60's to mid 70's. We had a three bedroom house, with three of our own kids then. I'd take in another three foster children. The rules were very different then and they would sometimes be brought in during the night. I would just put a pillow at the other end of my kids' beds and put them top to tail. In the morning I'd go in, and they would all be playing together. One big happy family, which it still is!

So I can't see me stopping working here, as I feel like a fish out of water when I'm not here. My husband John is still involved, in that he supplies the ice cream from the Company where he works, and he also does the stock orders. I hope retirement is a very long way off yet, as I enjoy meeting so many lovely people here.

GEOFF WILKINSON, WANSTEAD.

PROFESSIONAL PHOTOGRAPHER SINCE 1963.

Most of the teachers at my school in Stratford didn't know how to make their subjects interesting, but that was a lesson in itself - how NOT to teach! The only interesting teachers were in Geography and Art. I think that was the first hook of inspiration to see the world, and create images, but before that I had the serious business of having fun, playing with friends in the exposed cellars of a huge 2nd World War bomb site opposite our family flat, pretending, of course, to be soldiers!

But alongside that and cycling, aged eleven, I discovered the joy of making images with my parents' Brownie Box camera. The pictures that I took of my mates posing, and our holiday snaps, were very small when they came back from the Chemist, so I made a darkroom in my bedroom, and loved seeing the images come alive in the trays, until the smell of the chemicals drove me back out into the light! I actually won my first photography competition at thirteen, as a result of school trips abroad, fortunately for me, funded by my parents. That really got me hooked.

At fifteen, my first income came from a photo I took of Brian Poole, back at our old school, which was published on the front page of the Stratford Express. One guinea. That's £1.05. I left school as fast as possible, and started as a runner at a Photographic Agency in Fleet Street, then into the darkroom for two pasty skinned years, cleaning up photos for publication in the newspapers.

The Agency then sent me to take action photos at First Division football matches with my Halina camera, until I saved enough to buy a Rolleiflex, with the help of my lovely fiancee, Lyn. I was promoted to Editor, which was the highest available job there, so then I went to the Daily Mail every day, and pestered them until I was accepted on to their night shift, to cover film premieres and murders!! It was at that time that I got an exclusive photo of Princess Anne, on stage with the naked cast of Hair. (She kept her clothes on!) An exclusive that went all over the world meant that I was gaining a reputation.

In those days, the stars of stage and screen used to come looking for the camera, and I happily photographed many famous people. I moved to the Sun and at the same time, helped the BBC set up a library of still images. I always seemed to have two jobs, and as a result, hardly ever saw Lyn, who by now, in my early 20's, I had married. We were moved out to Florida by The National Enquirer where I worked as a Picture Editor. They had an amazing budget. I remember they hired a commercial airliner, to bring back just six rolls of film from a scoop that we had in South Africa.

We came back to the UK with Lyn expecting our daughter Danielle, and I was offered a job at the Sunday Mirror. Life got very exciting, but exhausting, living in airports and hotels all round the world, and working in conflicts and with guerillas who might have been hostile. We never could tell, so we always had Plan B - 'know where the nearest border was'! We recorded some very upsetting images of refugees in Honduras and wanted to help, but it was an impossible task. All we could do was tell the world and it was great that twenty of my images were used in one edition of that paper!

In 1986, after ten years of assignments including covering conflicts in Northern Ireland, Beirut etc., I needed a quieter life for a while. I was offered a deal I couldn't refuse, working for 'You' magazine in London and simultaneously covering Europe for the American publication 'People' magazine. Quieter life?? I filled my passport with 47 countries, shooting feature stories, the famous, and organic veg farms, including Prince Charles' Highgrove Estate. 'You' was very big into organics. One day the Editor sent me to Calcutta, to visit Mother Theresa to get an image we had discussed. The magazine thought it better not to bother phoning ahead, but just knock on her door! Well, as we landed, she was taking off to visit the Pope in Rome! We felt we had to stay on to get a story and found an orphanage run by two young English volunteers. It was so hopeless for the children there, you wanted to cry, but again I had to make a record of it to bring home.

I had some really enjoyable shoots, and one that sticks in my mind was with Sophia Loren. I spent a day in her kitchen, making dough and pizzas with her, and singing songs in Italian. In my mind, the perfect recipe for a perfect image of a beautiful person.Then I decided to change pace and settle down and finally I got to know my wife after thirty eight years of travelling! We set up here five years ago, and I now love passing on as much knowledge as possible to students on the workshops we run, and unlike my school teachers, I try to make it interesting!

It all started when a chap came in and asked for help with his new fangled digital camera. I learned very quickly what a great medium digital was, but I do actually miss the whiff of the chemicals in the darkroom! I'm always busy, and I'm still so passionate about photography. It is said that Variety is the Spice of Life and for me this could not be more true. I've led a very privileged life, and one day when it's raining I will write my book.

MARIAN TEMPLE, WANSTEAD.

CHARITY FUNDRAISER SINCE 1978.

I grew up in Aldersbrook Road with Wanstead Flats as my front garden, and Wanstead Park as my back garden. The cows trundled in and ate everything in the garden, and I thought that was normal! I walked to Aldersbrook Primary School each day, crossing the road on to the turf of the Flats, and imagined I was on a horse, galloping across the prairie. It took my mind off the fact I didn't like school, which was too noisy and competitive for my liking.

Later, I went to West Hatch High School, which was too big for me. Our home life was strongly influenced by the fact that my elder brother was disabled, and my parents were careful to reduce sibling competition as much as possible. This dislike of competition has stayed with me throughout my life.

In general I didn't like school, and at West Hatch I wasn't made to feel that I had any talents, so it was bizarre that I trained as a teacher, and then loved the job! It took me around all ages, many subjects, and a few countries, which made me curious about other cultures. I also wanted to satisfy this travel bug while I could, as I assumed I would be my brother's carer later in life.

My first long trip was the Kibbutz experience, which coincided with the outbreak of the Yom Kippur war. My parents typically allowed me to make the decision to stay and I made many long term friends and gained confidence in life, following my negative school experiences.

Later, while teaching in Greece, I was aware of their pre-democratic regime where torture was the norm. I was so privileged to have been born at the right time in a safe culture, and this awareness greatly influenced my future life. On my return to the UK in 1978, I joined Amnesty International, the Human Rights organisation formed in the 1960's from a Quaker background. Amnesty works in the murkiest corners of injustice around the globe.

I was a speaker for them, and visited schools and other organisations. I really wanted people to know what we were dealing with and would begin my talk with, "The first thing Sharmil's parents knew of their daughter's plight, was when the police called them, and ordered them to come and collect her body." This was a student on a demonstration, arrested, tortured and killed by the police in captivity. The police denied responsibility.

Such injustice galvanised me and other Amnesty members locally to organise events to raise funds to battle such regimes. Our local groups have probably raised some £50,000 over the years. Big events, and small donations for sales of homemade cards, jams and plants mount up over time.

I put a self service stall in my front garden in 1982 and started selling plants I had grown in my garden. I'm constantly delighted by the honesty of people who put their money through the letterbox. With the help of friends, I've thoroughly enjoyed opening my garden to the public for 15 years. Up to 80 people will come through the gate on a fine day, see the garden full of old fashioned flowers, and buy plants, home made jams and enjoy tea and homemade cakes. This year saw a record. We took a total of over £1000, all of it going to Amnesty International. I was overwhelmed – and exhausted!

Many of my plants have made their way up to the Corner House (Age UK) garden on the High Street, opposite the Co-op. I took that on in 2003 under the auspices of the Wanstead Society as it looked very sad and I felt I could cheer it up. With other volunteers I also enjoy doing the flower beds in the High Street, which I think makes a difference for the community.

Fundraising is something I do every day and I can't imagine giving it up as it's very satisfying. There might be the endless making of jams and chutneys for sale as part of my Amnesty Jamnesty campaign, but it keeps me warm in the kitchen in winter, and saves my heating bills! I don't sit down much and am very happy that way.

In fact, I'm just generally very happy!

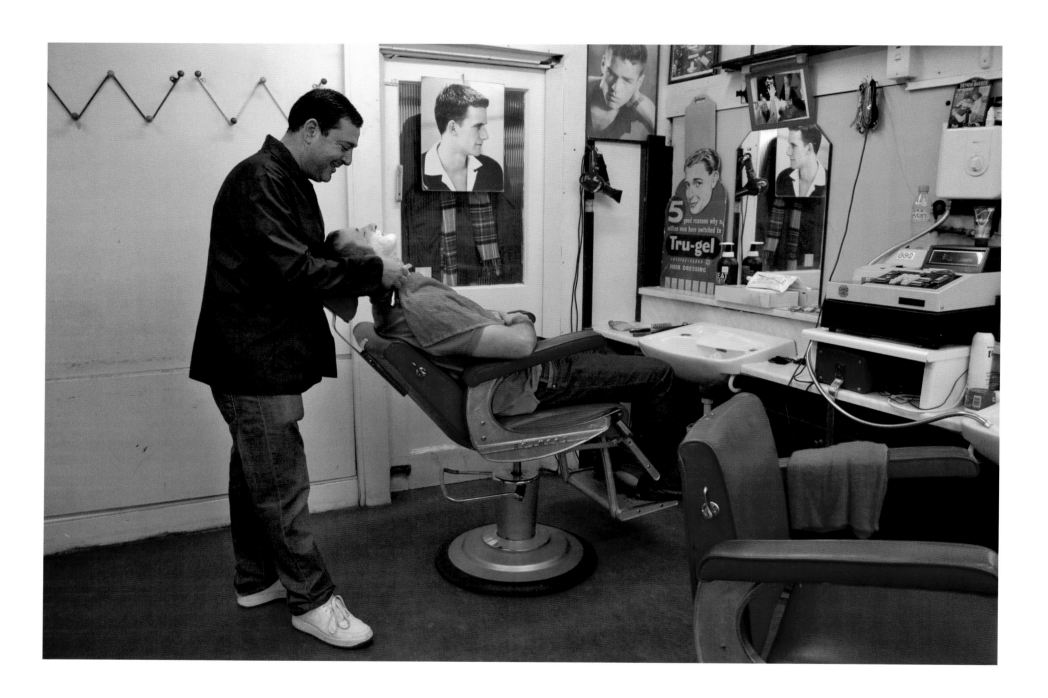

WANSTEAD HAIRDRESSERS, SINCE ABOUT 1940.

PAUL MICHAELIDES' FAMILY, HAIRDRESSERS SINCE 1969.

I was born in Wanstead in 1971, and went to local schools but I helped my Dad, who was by then in the 'Rag Trade', in the East End, buying and selling 'cabbages'! No, not the vegetable, but the insiders' name for the excess garments made by big manufacturers!

But both Mum and Dad, and my Uncle Steve were all hairdressers at one time, and so Dad pushed me into the business when I was eighteen, to get me away from cabbages, I think! I worked my way around several shops in East London, gaining a very useful apprenticeship, before coming here seventeen years ago to work for Uncle Steve, who had bought this business back in 1969. In fact, even though I bought the business from him, he still came in to cut some hair up to a year ago when he was in his late 70's.

As far as we know, apart from a short time as an office, this building has been a hairdressers for about seventy years. I've got a photo* obviously taken many, many years before that, which shows these premises were then an empty space between two buildings, which were part of a stable block, so effectively, it was an early day brownfield site urban infill!

I have to make the distinction that we are Barbers rather than Hairdressers, despite the sign outside! We often joke that you need another trim two weeks after seeing a hairdresser, but as we cut a bit closer, our cuts last longer. But seriously, we all do a good job, just serving a slightly different market. Funnily enough, one customer whose friend was taking the mickey out of him, saying he was being posh, brought him along to show him the sign to prove he went to a Hairdressers!

Mind you, the star of the show in our shop are these Belmont Appolo chairs, which as far as I believe were made in the '30's and are still working beautifully. They were certainly here when Uncle Steve moved in, and are obviously the sturdy antique version rather than modern reproductions. They cope with a huge number of backsides every week, small and large, year in year out, don't complain, get lots of compliments, and still look lovely!!

When I was very young, helping out here, I wondered what my Uncle was selling to customers on a Friday from the tray marked Durex which was under the counter. But I don't remember him asking the famous phrase "Anything for the weekend sir?"! Barbers were a real mens' preserve in those days, perhaps up to about the early 1980's. Condoms, the odd 'mens' magazine, and male banter. Women wouldn't even consider stepping inside. That's all changed of course, but we still have plenty of banter and laughter, especially as I've known most of my customers for years, and some are friends in the area. I do get some customers moaning about the missus as well. Perhaps that's why, if a woman comes in, the conversation does change slightly. For obvious reasons I won't repeat those stories.

I think it's a male thing to stick to the devil you know, because I have many, very loyal customers. In fact, I still have a couple of elderly chaps who used to have their hair cut at my Dad's shop in Stepney, donkeys' years ago before they moved to this area. They came in here not realising the shop was run by the same family, but have come back here ever since. Indeed, Dad used to have his hair cut by Uncle Steve, and he wouldn't even let me near him with a pair of scissors until Uncle finally hung his up for good! I think he trusts me now.

We still get queues of customers out the door on a Saturday, and despite there being more competition around, we always seem to have had a good steady flow of work. I always say that we can't possibly cut everyones' hair in Wanstead so I think we'll be here for years to come.

Despite now living further out, I love this area, and the very friendly relationship I have with my customers, and other people I know who still live here. But as I'm on my feet all day talking, listening, enjoying and concentrating on my work, I'm very happy to go home to a quiet life after work.

* From Epping Forest Then and Now. Ramsey and Fowkes.

JOHN EYRE, CHURCH BELL RINGER.

BELL TOWER KEEPER SINCE 1955, CHRIST CHURCH, WANSTEAD.

I've not moved far from where I was born in Chingford in 1939. After being schooled locally, I went to work for the Bank of England in the City, then after two years National Service, I returned to the Bank and was posted to their Printing Works in Loughton, where I worked for the next twenty seven years. In 1988 I was seconded to coordinate the work of the Prince's Youth Business Trust, in Essex.

Over the next ten years I helped unemployed and disadvantaged young people in Essex explore the option of self employment. The counselling involved the preparation of business plans, training and market research followed by exposure to a board of highly qualified business personnel. Successful applicants with the right spark could obtain a loan or a grant from the Trust and were introduced to a mentor. It was very rewarding, as I helped many young people start their own business, and I believe the hundreds more that I counselled were appreciative of my efforts and found that the whole experience had made them more employable.

But that takes me away from the point of this story. In 1955, when I moved to Wanstead, a school friend of mine who was a choirboy at Christ Church, told me that if I joined the church, he would allocate me a girlfriend rather than have me pinch one of his. He was true to his word, as I met Sheila, who I later married, and we recently celebrated our Golden Wedding. We attend church regularly, but I admit that back then, I was probably more interested in the opposite sex than religion!

There wasn't any room in the choir for me, but there was a vacancy as a bell ringer. Also, the man who maintained the bells above our heads, the bell tower keeper, was suffering with his health, and was having difficulty crawling up through small trapdoors and over the bells, so at the age of sixteen I offered to take his place. I have been crawling through small spaces ever since, checking ropes and pulleys high above the town, silently tending to the needs of eight brooding brazen maidens.

I have also taught bell management to many people of all ages from many walks of life. As a bell ringer, it takes about six weeks to learn how to control the bell and then ring in with your fellow band of ringers. Good bell control is important, as our big bell generates enough force through the rope to lift a small van, so letting go at the right time is vital, to avoid bodily contact with the ceiling!

There then follows a lifetime of learning various methods thereby practicing the art of Change Ringing. This combines teamwork with the ability for the individual to target their own desired levels of accomplishment. Change Ringing originated in England some 400 years ago and over the centuries, bells have proclaimed the presence of the Church in the community, summoned to worship, rung for weddings and important occasions, and tolled for funerals. A warm welcome awaits visiting bell ringers in almost all the ringing chambers in the country, whether they are church goers or not, so I feel we are a rather special breed of people. Our own weekly bell practice concludes with a quiz night at the Nightingale (p.7) - a perfect end to the day.

The first ring of six bells at Christ Church was installed in 1869. The benefactor at the time stipulated they be made of steel, which I'm afraid makes a horrid sound, like scaffolding being dismantled. Fortunately for us now, they rusted and were replaced with a bronze set in 1934. In 1972, two further bells were added to complete the octave, and thereby hangs a tale. A choir member, with whom we bantered over his utter dislike of all things to do with ringing, had bequeathed a sum of money to be spent on the church organ upon his death, which occurred tragically early. However, the organ had only just been overhauled, so the Church consulted his family, who agreed to fund the installation of a new bell frame and the casting of two new bells, with his name preserved forever, inscribed thereon in Latin! I'm sure he would have been totally bemused but delighted with the outcome of his beneficence!

As for my future in the Tower, well, as my knees are creaking a bit these days, I am training a very able apprentice to take over the maintenance, but I fully intend to carry on ringing bells in perpetuity.

JUDITH ZIMELSTERN, WANSTEAD.

OWNER, JUDITH OF WANSTEAD, EST. 1977.

My father ran away from home when he was eleven years old, fended for himself, and later made a good life for himself, so he decided that formal further education was unnecessary. So, there I was, born into this Jewish family in Goodmayes just after the end of the 2nd World War. I absolutely loved school. I was very academic, in the top stream and also loved sport, playing netball for Essex. I was Head Girl at William Talbot, moved on to Beale County High, and then Dad pulled the carpet from under my feet by taking me out of education at fifteen to work in his dress manufacturing business. I was absolutely devastated.

Despite my protestations, he trained me to manage his factory, but I hated it. I was doing some sketching and designing, and had an eye for that part of the work, and I wanted to study Design at Central St. Martin's College of Art and Design, but again, Dad refused. In many other ways, he was wonderful to me, so I stuck at the work for fourteen years. By then I had been married, had two children, got divorced, and was struggling to make ends meet so I worked part time for my Dad's close friend Laurie Schramm and his wonderful wife, Arlene.

I was taking sample ranges to retailers, and I brought in a lot of new business, and even had dealings with the chief buyer from Iran, which was a massive coup. One day in 1977, Laurie told me that he would back me if I wanted to go into business on my own. That was an offer I couldn't refuse, so the very next morning, I went out and found some available premises in Wanstead High Street.

Laurie came down and told me that my first choice, which was part of what is now Nicole's the card shop, was too small, and told me to take on these larger premises instead. It wasn't a good time for small shops, and everyone said I was mad to even think about it, but I reckoned that I could bring customers in, as long as I was selling the right product.

On the evening before the formal opening, there I was in the window, doing some last minute alterations to the mannequins, and there was a tap on the window. "Have you got that skirt in a size eight? I want to be your first customer." I did have that size, and Valerie Delin became my first customer, and she still buys her clothes here, thirty six years later! I was new to retail, and because of my background of scrimping and saving as a single Mum, I was amazed that someone was prepared to spend £27 on a skirt. It was a lot of money in those days.

It was a tough start, with little stock, but Laurie Schramm helped smooth the way, and word spread very effectively, eventually as far afield as Australia, Hong Kong, Africa and the Middle East. As well as women of all backgrounds from all over the UK wanting to look their best for weddings, parties and other ceremonies, customers from all over the world will come to me while they are visiting London. We help Greek, African, Jewish and Arab women look spectacular for their very glamorous functions. We have a number of celebrity customers, including radio presenters who are kind enough to have mentioned our name on the BBC.

When necessary, we make alterations to the dresses that the customers are buying, as they want to look their pristine best. So I take on board all the worry from the customer, which makes this a very high pressure job, but that's the sort of service they are paying for. Fortunately, I have had a wonderful partner for thirty seven years, Ron, who is my peace of mind at home at the end of the day. His support in all ways has been such that without him, I couldn't possibly have been successful. I've also been so lucky to have such a loyal, considerate staff and an outstanding business partner, Arlene Schramm, who all bring their own character to the business, and who have all become good friends.

We cater for sizes 8 to 26, and for women from the youthful to the elderly. I don't know of any other shops of this ilk anywhere near here, but we try to compete with the likes of Harrods and Fenwicks.

I wonder how those shops would have dealt with a well heeled customer of ours who came in regularly with her beautiful, treasured Afghan Hound. She would try a dress on and ask her dog if she liked it! If the dog barked, she would buy the dress, and if she looked disinterested, the dress went back on the hanger. We would try to keep the dog happy by feeding her chocolate treats, to encourage more barks when her owner emerged from the changing room! We must have been doing something right, because the dog and her owner returned to us again and again!

RICHARD WYBER, ASSOCIATE PRIEST, WANSTEAD.

ST. MARY'S CHURCH, WANSTEAD. BUILT 1790.

I was born in Bromley in 1947. My mother had been brought up as a Unitarian and was baptised as an adult into the Church of England, so the church became an important part of her life, whereas my father had no involvement. So I attended with her, and I'd like to think, because of her, and then when I went to study Economics and Law at Cambridge in the late 1960's, I continued as a regular worshipper.

Other parts of life then distracted me for some years, until I met my wife to be, Jean, at a Country Dance in 1979. I had found a good social life and a way of keeping relatively fit with a Morris Dancing group. I kept up the dancing for a good many years after that, until a dodgy knee halted me a few years ago.

Jean was brought up in the Congregational Church and after the birth of our sons in the mid '80's, she joined the United Free Church in Woodford Green. Initially I went along with her but then decided I wanted to be back in the Anglican Church. I think the traditional hymns we sang at school all those years before must have struck more than just a chord.

It then felt right to develop my involvement, so I started to help out at church services, carrying the cross, preparing the altar and reading lessons. Also, I led small groups which are held in people's houses. I liked the informality, and relaxed nature of these groups.

Come the late '90's I took a two year course in Christian Studies, during which time I felt a call to go further. Then, after a selection process and another three year course, I was ordained as Deacon at Chelmsford in 2006 and Priest in 2007. I was appointed Curate in the Parish of Wanstead, and now serve as an Associate Priest.

I like St.Mary's, with its long history. There has been a church on this site since medieval times. King James I visited Wanstead many times and was regularly in residence at Wanstead House and texts survive of a number of significant sermons preached at Wanstead Church in his presence. In 1790, the present church was built on the same site as the medieval church, using money and influences from the East India Company (the pulpit has some very oriental touches) and has served the local community ever since. St.Mary's is the only Grade 1 listed building in Redbridge.

The large, ornate statue behind the pulpit is that of Sir Josiah Child, (1630 -1699), who was the Governor of the Company in its early days, and who commisioned the magnificent gardens of Wanstead House. The statue occupies the same position as it did in the medieval church, although that must have looked odd, as that church was apparently small and basic. However, the present building does his statue justice. The index finger of his right hand can just be seen pointing downwards and in the Crypt below the church, directly in line with his finger, can be found a glass phial which contains his preserved heart!

We have a regular congregation here each week but I also enjoy taking services at Christ Church, behind Wanstead High Street, which has a somewhat different feel to it, and a larger congregation. I enjoy saying prayers with the bell ringers, under the captaincy of John Eyre, who is also in this book (p.43).

People ask whether I aspire to a parish of my own, but I am happy here, and don't feel I need to climb any more ladders. Most clergy continue at least until the age of 70, and often well beyond, so I hope to be here for some time! Jean has continued to be heavily involved at the United Free, and although there is, of course, no competition between our churches, we do enjoy debating the finer points of our different practices.

E4

Chingford &

Highams Park

DR. GEORGIE CAVE, WANSTEAD. GP SINCE 1992.

RIDGEWAY PRACTICE PARTNER, CHINGFORD SINCE 1999.

It's a great help as a GP to be able to get on well with people, and to be able to assess and understand their character. That's where my Mum comes in! As the eldest daughter of a vicar and his wife, living in Jamaica in a large house with maids, she could twist her dad round her little finger. She has always been a feisty woman who can see straight through you. Coming to the UK on The Windrush, she claims to have been the only person on that boat to be wearing fur coat and boots, ready for a British winter, and also to look glamorous! I'd like to think these characteristics of being prepared and being able to understand people have rubbed off on me. Perhaps even appreciating a bit of glamour.

As well as following her nursing career, she raised seven children in straightened circumstances in Brixton. Dad died when I was three years old but she coped so well. She believes that you gain independence through education and made sure that we all went to University. She went on to get involved in local politics and became a school governor, and is also regarded as a Queen of Brixton Market where she has always shopped. She still cooks as if she has seven children living with her, but there will always be one of us popping by to enjoy her food!

But, back to me! I was studious at school but had a mischievous streak, getting involved in some St.Trinians' style pranks for which I never got caught. I found my initial interest in Chemistry at an all girls school at about fifteen years old then when we joined the Boys School in the 6th Form, we were the only two girls in the Chemistry class with loads of less mature boys. We decided to sit at the front to stop the irritation of them trying to distract us. My friend drove a motorbike to school in full leathers, sometimes with me on pillion in full school uniform and we could distract the boys by acting slightly haughty as we walked past them. Poor boys!

Like my Mum, I was interested in what made people tick, and I was heading towards Psychiatry until a Careers Adviser told me that the medical world would be too difficult to pursue. That made my mind up even more, and over the next nine years I studied all the disciplines of health and qualified to become a GP. As a junior doctor on the long sleepless weekend shifts, you had to learn to take two minute naps whilst standing and still be able to have a good laugh, otherwise you'd never survive! Having a good team of people around you was a real bonus for mutual support and banter and I encountered some wonderful, hard working, devoted people over the years.

In 1990, I met Frank, a trainee surgeon, and as we became more involved with each other, (eventually to marry) I was very happy to follow him to Birmingham to start my life as a Locum GP in 1992. A few years later, I happily returned to Practice in my old stomping ground as I had had a wonderful GP mentor in South London who, after all the theory, had taught me about life as a GP. One day, after I had explained to a patient all about hormones, sex drive and HRT, she said, with a suck of the teeth and a raised eyebrow, "And how is your mother, Georgieana?" So despite my qualifications and experience, I was still 'Mrs.Jackson's daughter from Brixton'. It made me feel really grounded and aware of my roots. It was a special moment for me.

Home visits over the years threw up all sorts of tricky situations, sometimes scary ones at night on my own. I carried all my gear in a hard case, as I figured I could use it for self protection if necessary. Just taking a patient's blood pressure readings could provoke a reaction in a protective dog, something some dog owners didn't appreciate. Fortunately, I never had to use the case! And I had some funny emergency calls late at night when I was on call. "I can't get the dentures out of my Mum's mouth". Leave them in till morning? But, of course, all calls have to be taken seriously, however tired or sleep deprived you are.

And so to my present Practice in Chingford, which is a short commute from my home in Wanstead, and where I think I will see out my GP years. I am now seeing the grown offspring of my original patients, and it's interesting to note that it's common for them to respond to illness in a similar way to their parents, which can be of help to me! Many patients have also seen or heard about my children growing up, so that all helps the relationship. Fortunately I can also enjoy laughing with a patient. Once, I 'lectured' an elderly gentleman on the importance of the various drugs which he was supposed to be taking, and when I finished he said "And here endeth the sermon." He looked so serious that I just cracked up, and we enjoyed a good laugh together.

I think the laughter helps me stay sane – after all, I'm still here! And recently, I read a paper which asserted that, for a woman, the most desirable professional male is a surgeon, but for a man, the least desirable professional woman is a GP!! I'm married to a surgeon – I win!

JOYCE NICHOLLS. CHINGFORD.

KEEP FIT TEACHER SINCE 1960.

I teach four classes every week these days, the biggest one being twenty to twenty five strong. All women! I remember one man started at my class in Theydon Bois. He didn't last..... But one class which has stood the test of time is my over 60's class on a Thursday. I have a very loyal group, four of whom are in their 90's! They all come to me at a church hall, and we do some seated, and standing movements to keep them fit and agile.

It was in 1956 that I started going to keep fit classes, under the banner of the Keep Fit Association. My teacher at the time suggested I should be a teacher as well, so I took the plunge and trained up in about 1960. We always had a lot of fun, including performing with the Eastern Counties Region at the annual events at the Albert Hall. I remember choreographing one performance with forty women in the group, to the 'March Militaire' by Schubert. One year, we went to Denmark and represented the England KFA, but I stayed well clear of the choreography for that one!! By the way, absolutely no men were involved!

Anatomy and movement had always interested me, and back in the '40's, while my future husband was away working at Sheffield University, I trained as a Physiotherapist, qualifying in 1948 at the London Hospital in Whitechapel, one week before the National Health Service started. It was a predominantly Jewish area at the time, and I recall lots of, shall we say, rotund Jewish ladies with dodgy joints, who enjoyed the massage techniques we used, but weren't so keen to do the follow up remedial exercises!

I worked part time in Pre-natal Preparation, while having three of my own babies, then went full time at Whipps Cross maternity in 1981. Then in 1992, aged sixty five, I tried to retire, but realised I was still enjoying the work, so went back part time for another five years until I wasn't allowed to work any longer because of age regulations. During that time I ran one particular post-natal physio group class, which stayed together and formed the Keep Fit class in the photo, which is still running every Wednesday!

I don't have any plans to stop teaching, as it helps me keep fit and well. Mind you, I am often told 'You can't stop teaching, where would we be without you?'

The exercise keeps my brain fit as well, I'm absolutely sure of that. After I've had a couple of hours walk in the morning with my husband (he's not too keen on exercise, but he knows it does him good), I do a Sudoku puzzle and a crossword or two. Years ago I responded to a Mensa test in the newspaper, and got accepted! Fortunately, it's not a test of memory, but it's all about logic. I still get the Mensa Newsletters, but don't usually bother to read them. Actually I don't really have time, what with a woman's work at home, three children and seven grandchildren to keep up with, and trying to keep pace with modern technology. I generally get to bed about midnight, and after seven hours sleep, I have another full day to deal with.
All three of my children have been involved in the health sector in their work, as a Paediatrician, a GP, and a PE teacher respectively. I'm not sure if it's my influence or not! My son, the GP, has now retired at the age of sixty. Now that makes me feel a bit odd!

So does this – I've been awarded the British Empire Medal in recognition of services to Keep Fit in Essex. Following the acceptance of the medal at a ceremony at the Tower of London, I'm looking forward to meeting the Queen at the Garden Party at Buckingham Palace next summer!!

HEALES CYCLES, CHINGFORD SINCE 1937.

ASHLEY MORGAN – PARTNER SINCE 1996.

I loved bikes as a kid, and bought my first one with my paper round money. I was twelve, and I remember it was a bright yellow, five speed racer which I bought from Haires of Bath, where I was brought up. After I started tinkering with its mechanics, I got hold of second hand ones, and used the parts to build new ones for myself. Then I joined Bath Cycling Club, and rode and raced my bikes on the local roads.

Bath didn't do it for me as a youth, and having left an unsatisfactory school life behind at fifteen, drifting through various jobs with my dad pushing me all the way, I left home – twice! At seventeen I got a City and Guilds in Mechanics whilst on day release from a Motor mechanics apprenticeship, and my last job in Bath was in customer reception work at BMC, which became British Leyland, which became.....nothing!

Whilst at BMC in 1983, I was in a long distance relationship with Pauline, who I later married, and I heard about a job at a garage in Winchmore Hill. That scenario made it very easy to break my ties with Bath, and two weeks later I moved in with Pauline's parents in Southgate. But again, after a while I started to drift jobs, but always in the motor trade, for the next ten years. I also drifted away from all forms of exercise, including cycling.

Pauline and I got married and moved to Highams Park, where I found Heales Cycles and rediscovered bikes, and fitness. Heales was owned by Colin Geyman, and one day when I was buying bike bits in 1994, he mentioned that he had to find a new mechanic. I was in middle management at VW at the time, disenchanted as usual. I went outside, sat in my company Audi, thought about this for a minute or two, and decided I could do the job. Colin asked me to come for an interview so, after discussing finances with Pauline, and assuring her we could live on a third of my old salary, I went in on the next Saturday. Interview – what interview – I just fixed a dodgy bike, then another, then another. Then I was hired!

Two years later, the offer of becoming a partner in the business came up. I reckoned that with my marketing background I could sell sand to the Arabs so, again with Pauline's consent, in I went. We took Heales from a business which was ticking over, to a higher end retailer by taking advantage of the launch of a new range of quality bikes by the manufacturer Marin. It proved to be a success.

Heales had first opened its doors here in 1937, with Lionel Heales expertly welding frames in his foundry out the back, and constructing wheels, while his wife Winn used her half of the shop to sell haberdashery! They were both members of Victoria Cycling Club, lived above the shop all their lives and after Lionel died in 1987, Winn carried on the business until she died in 1991.

So, with such a long history, I wanted to keep Heales working well for the local cyclists, and after Colin hung up his bike clips in 1999, I went halves in the business with Dennis. The days of welding frames have long gone, although the foundry chimney is still there, but we stock a very impressive range of off road, and hybrid bikes. For a while, Trevor Maddern occupied a small corner of the shop selling road bikes, until he opened his own shop, Ciclos Uno in Hainault.

Back in 1997, we were the first cycle shop to organise group rides into Epping Forest. We called the events 'Heales Sunday rides'. How imaginative! But they have been very popular, and also brought in a lot of new business for us. On the first run, it was me and one other person, but I persevered and it grew to thirty five strong at it's zenith. Unfortunately two years ago, my knees had had enough, and my doctor told me to only ride gently! I don't do gently, so I don't take part any more.

We get a huge range of people coming into the shop, and we try to accommodate all-comers – from the blokes who want to be one up on their mates, to the chaps who know the exact gearings they want, and which they can discuss for hours. Every customer is different. I still feel a bit sorry for the youngsters who come in with their Dads, drooling over a top of the range model, but having to accept something cheaper. Mind you, once they grow up, then they can choose what to spend their own money on.

And now Pauline has given her consent again – this time to become a co-Director with me. My business partner Dennis has hung up his bike clips, so Pauline and I are now co-Directors and as such we have become a family business, just as it was in the days of Mr and Mrs Heales. We'll keep the name Heales, but I haven't yet asked Pauline if she wants half the shop for haberdashery!!!

BOB CLARK, NATURE LOVER FOR 50 YEARS.

PROPRIETOR, SECOND NATURE WHOLEFOOD SHOP SINCE 1990. WOOD STREET E17.

Ever since I can remember I have been interested in nature. I'm sure every kid enjoys peering into rock pools at the beach, but every year of my childhood my family went to Brixham, and as a small boy I realised how much variety of life was to be seen in those little pools of mystery. I then carried that realisation into adulthood, always appreciating that whatever we do to the planet, it will eventually have an effect on our lives.

I was born in Walthamstow at the end of the 50's, went to school locally, and my first job was at my brother's butcher's shop. Then I took a year out, travelling and living a bit rough around Scotland, which was like an holistic version of National Service. I think everyone should be encouraged to do it, because it was certainly a character building experience. When I returned, I became a roadie with a New Romantic band in the 80's. That lasted a couple of years, followed by a bit more butchery, and then some gardening.

In 1990, I decided I had to get a proper job, so the long hair went, but not my 'hippie' ideals. As I said earlier, I had always had great respect for the planet, and I also had experience of organic gardening. It was difficult finding food products that would suit my daughter, who had some food intolerances at the time. So it was a natural progression to come into this business with my partner at that time.

The common phrase 'second nature' appealed to us as a title of a business, because if you can't get what you want from nature first hand, then come to us! So, we started selling from home, then quickly moved into the indoor market in Wood Street, where the rents were very cheap.

We took the opportunity to rent these premises fifteen years ago. It was previously an Antiques shop, and before that, a butcher's. Some of my older customers remember animals being kept out the back, in a small pasture, which has disappeared under relatively modern housing. In fact, these premises are Grade II listed, as 'an eighteenth century weatherboarded butcher's shop'. They had their own slaughterhouse, as did most small butchers in those days. Having worked in a butcher's, I can picture the scene, with carcasses rather than bags of onions hanging from hooks outside the shop. A far cry from the vegetarian produce I sell nowadays!

This is the only shop of its kind in quite a large area, so customers come from a fair distance. I think they represent the whole gamut of life, and can spend twenty minutes or more chatting with other customers. The most common phrase I overhear is "I didn't realise you shopped here"! So it's a great meeting place and I feel it's putting something back into the local community as well as the wider world. We have requests for cigarettes, phone cards and rat poison, but most of all, body building supplements. But they are not our bag at all. We specialise in fresh and packaged foods, either selling from here, or delivering locally.

Away from here, I enjoy sketching, poetry, fishing, walking and cooking, and I keep my own bees, all of which helps me feel closer to nature.

RON VOWDEN, SHOE REPAIRER SINCE 1959.

RON'S SHOE REPAIRS, CHINGFORD. EST 1976.

I was born in Devon in 1947, and was adopted. Sadly, my new mum died when I was six years old, so I spent my young life with my adopted dad. He had been disabled as a child by measles, and basically grew up in hospital and even learned his trade as a cobbler whilst in there! I continually moved all over Devon with him as he looked for work in appropriate premises, and I went to sixteen different schools, never quite fitted in, and was bullied as a permanent new boy. So I didn't get a great education, and can still struggle with writing skills.

But that hasn't held me back, because my memory is good and my hands are skilled. I worked in my Dad's shops from when I was twelve years old, until I finished school. My first job was repairing big old heavy army boots. I came to North London with Dad and then got married in 1973. At the time I was working for a nationwide heel bar company, ending up as Area Manager, in charge of sixteen shops, and thirty two staff.

My wife and I moved to Chingford, and in 1976 I decided that I'd had enough of the long hours without overtime pay, and driving long distances, so I decided I'd rather use the hours to run my own business. This place came up for sale in 1976. It had been a shoe repairers (R.Boyle) since 1934, so was well established. '76 was the hot summer, and the first thing I had to do was replace the windows, as the small panes cracked in the extreme heat. As you can imagine, inside the shop it was unbearable!

I have had up to four people working here, and it was a bit of a squeeze, but I'm on my own now, as far more people throw shoes away nowadays, despite the fact that they have perfectly good uppers and just need a cheap repair to the heel or the sole. Mind you, the other day I worked out that since I started working at twelve years old, I have been involved in the repair of close on one million pairs of shoes, so I'm not too fussed that business is slowing a bit!!!

Most of my work comes in by word of mouth. Some work comes in by post from a distance, and one job came from as far away as Nigeria. That was a strange one. I repaired the shoes, but before I could send them back, I got a message that the owner of the shoes had died. I had already been paid and was asked to dispose of the shoes. Another time, a Canadian lady who lived locally, brought in a shopping trolley with broken wheels. I fixed them for her, and we became friends for about the last ten years of her life. Later, I received a letter from her daughter in Canada saying how much her mum had enjoyed our friendship. That was really touching, as was the unsigned greeting card I received recently, congratulating me for 35 years of business here. Now who would remember something like that? (Actually it was a year early, at 34 years, but that's beside the point!)

I like to support charities, so I have these collection boxes here, and over the years, through my customers' generosity, I've been able to pass on £10,000 to the Guide Dogs for the Blind, and £4,000 to St.Francis Hospice.
Outside of here, I have one day off a week, and use that to do the books, but I manage to enjoy working and relaxing in the garden. I have no plans for the future, other than to carry on working while my health allows, so I can carry on enjoying meeting and helping my customers.

STEVE SANDLER, DO. PhD., CHINGFORD.

OSTEOPATH SINCE 1975.

Why Osteopathy? Well, when I was dating a young woman, I turned up at her house, and she could hardly walk as she was in so much pain with her back. Then, a week later, there seemed to have been a miracle. How on earth had she recovered so quickly, I asked. The answer was that she had been treated by an Osteopath. I was intrigued, and hooked.

But lets go back a few years to my childhood. In 1950 I was born in the East End and I remember living in a prefab in the Cambridge Heath Road, until the family moved up in the world into a Council House in Hackney where I stayed until I got married. I was lucky enough to thoroughly enjoy my schooling at what was then a Grammar School for Boys, where the teachers wore gowns, but were utterly inspiring. Especially the Science teacher, who encouraged us to have inquiring minds. From that moment, I was interested in the living form, and thence Human Anatomy. But as students of Science, we also had to spend one afternoon a week studying the Arts. This was immense fun, including being led round the school corridors by the Art teacher who was playing violin, and we followed him singing Russian folk songs with gusto! Great days.

And so to University, where I studied Dentistry for two years, until I realised I didn't want to spend the rest of my life being hated by people! I also disliked the idea of working in the hierarchy of General Medical practice, so I was fortunate that my girlfriend hurt her back at about the same time! My Dad was a taxi driver at the time, so there wasn't a lot of money available, but he encouraged me to pursue my dream, which entailed a four year course of study at the British School of Osteopathy (BSO).

I popped in there to have a look on a Friday in 1971, enrolled to start training on the next Monday, and you could say the rest is history. It was the best decision I ever made. I was taught by some of the greats in the business at that time, and the year I qualified, there were 11 of us studying. Keep that figure in your mind for a moment.

One of the tutors, Colin Dove, took me under his wing, and I started working at his Practice in Romford as soon as I qualified in 1975. But he also insisted that I should teach at the BSO, and despite a few nerves, I started that part of my career just three months later. I loved it, and rose through the ranks to a senior position, and helped transform the BSO from a small organisation, to one which is known worldwide. Now there are 500 students a year rather than 11, and it is the biggest clinic of its kind in the world, where students practice under strict supervision. I also opened a facility to treat Expectant Mothers, which was the first of its kind. Now, most large practices and teaching establishments have an Expectant Mothers Clinic.

This came as a result of my inquiring mind which gave rise to a very long study into Obstetrics, pregnancy, and ligament and joint laxity at certain times during the menstrual cycle. In all, eleven years of research which led to a Doctorate, but it's enabled me to work in an area I find inspiring, and very fulfilling. This also led me to have a Practice at the Portman Hospital.

But in all honesty, my whole career has been fulfilling. An Osteopath isn't just a joint manipulator. That only takes three seconds. An Osteopath will listen, and evaluate the health of the whole person, and treat accordingly. So many issues can cause pain, from stress, illness, and poor posture at work, to emotional turmoil, and physical injury. These issues need to be addressed, not only at the point of the pain presented, but on a much deeper level. I want to ask some patients when they last bit someone, as they come in with their shoulders round their ears, similar to a dog with it's hackles up – an anger response, and a warning of an impending snap at your heels! But, obviously, I keep it calm, and with touch, help to restore fluidity of movement, and improved overall health.

My teachings in twenty countries across Europe has opened my mind to different ways of working, so Osteopathy is a constantly evolving practice, and has attained legality in many countries since the UK Parliament recognised the profession in 1993. I have no reason to stop work, as it brings me such pleasure, and there are times I would happily pay, rather than be paid, to see the reaction of people who are released from pain.

An old East Ender summed it up for me. He really needed a new hip, but was ineligible for surgery. He came to see me every month for many years and one day said "Nah Steve, you'n me are gunna die, right? But I wanna die furst, 'cos if you go furst an ain't arahnd no more, oo's gunna look after me?" It so happened that his wish was fulfilled, but I can have the privilege of continuing to care.

MICK O'DWYER, WANSTEAD AND CHINGFORD.

FARRIER SINCE 1953.

I think my Dad was disappointed that when I left Secondary school in 1947 in Co.Tipperary, I became a 'man of deeds' whereas my brother was a 'man of words'. You see, I had always preferred being out in the countryside with the dogs, and had hung around one of my Uncle Maurice's forges since I was a kid, so I learned the blacksmith's trade. Actually, my Dad was devastated! But I wanted to earn some money, so I could treat myself, amongst other things, to the occasional wet shave at my local barbers. Guess how much that cost in 1947. Thruppence ha'penny! That's two pence in new money!

In 1953 I finished my training as a blacksmith making horseshoes, and then as a farrier, that's a man who 'nails up' the shoes on the horses, and got jobs locally for a while.

Then, in 1956 I came to England through Liverpool, and within six months of arriving in London I was married. To an Irish girl! As a general blacksmith I worked in the Earls Court Road, making lots of gates during the post war rebuilding years. I moved around for a few years, including working for Edmonton Council, then decided to leave in 1968 on the advice of a friend who has greyhounds. He told me of the demand for farriers.

It's been a real tough job, and I've got my aches and pains, so now, at over eighty years old, I help out at some local stables, but not too much with the big horses any more. They are too strong and heavy. But because I left the Council, I don't get a pension, so I can't put my feet up just yet. (I shouldn't have listened to my friend!)

You know I was thinking, my Dad said I am a 'man of deeds', but at the stables I always seem to have the last word! Mind you, who'd argue with me, with a hammer in one hand, and a rasp in the other! But I also love a well written poem, and they can make me quite melancholy too. Sadly, my first wife died long ago, but I remarried twenty years ago, and have a couple of teenagers at home. They keep me on my toes.

There's a couple of other characters in this book that I recognise, Sue at Chapmans the Butchers (p73). I shod her horses for a while in the 70's, and Ron the Cobbler in North Chingford who I have been friends with for years (p59). As lovely as he is, I'm not sure why after all these years he still calls me Colin. My name's always been Mick in England, and to all my family I was known as 'Mickle'!

Like the words of the French singer, Edith Piaf, I have 'no regrets'.

HEATHER UTTERIDGE, CHINGFORD. OPTOMETRIST SINCE 1977.

OWNER, VICKERY AND UTTERIDGE LTD, SINCE 1987.

My mother taught me in a very unusual way to strive to do my best. She was a schizophrenic and regularly attacked me verbally, emotionally and physically, and constantly belittled me, so I had to get very strong very quickly or go under, and I decided I had to be the best at everything I tried. So, at the age of eight I employed the services of the biggest boy in school to help me deal with a bully. It worked, and my learning curve began. I then managed to persuade my mother not to use any more violence against me, but I'd rather not say how I achieved that! My Dad was always away, so as a child I found myself running the house, finding cash to pay the bills, finding the offices to hand the cash over, doing the washing, ironing etc.

I loved my senior school despite coming from a different background from the other girls, but I quietly stuck up for myself. The one subject that defeated me was music, and my teacher became so exasperated at my lack of interest, that in one lesson out of sheer frustration he threw a music stand out of the classroom window! Other than that I was in the top five percent, but still thought I was no good, so I gained the ability to forge school Parents Sign off Reports for the benefit of my ever critical mother.

For some reason, she wanted me to be a Physiotherapist, but I only lasted six months in the pompous hierarchies of Kings College. My character was forming and from then on, I made my own decisions about my future, and really enjoyed some time at Moorfields Eye Hospital. I lapped up information like there was no tomorrow and decided that eyes were for me. There followed years of study at various colleges to qualify as an Optician.

I met my first husband whilst at college, and together we set up practices in the City, but I saw Opticians with varying levels of talent, and a lack of understanding about the effects that prescription drugs could have on the eyes. I was intrigued by this link as I knew about medications from my Hospital days, so I became interested in Optometry. That involved years more study alongside potential GP's, but it was endlessly fascinating and really rewarding. An Optometrist will see, and diagnose many health issues through examination of the eyes, from leukemia to brain tumours, and from drug side effects to systemic problems such as diabetes and dyslexia.

For once, I didn't pass the exam first time. One of the examiners, unknown to me, was close behind me observing me check a patient with a squint. I was 'waving' my rod around for the patient to follow, and I whacked the examiner in the head! My marks were excellent, so it must have been the assault that failed me! But once I'd qualified in 1977, I did my year's pre-registration with the highly regarded Andrew Field here in Station Road, and when he retired in 1987, I bought his practice and established Vickery and Utteridge Ltd.

Suddenly, you are on your own, making decisions about observations and diagnoses, but confidence and knowledge grows, especially when if in doubt, you refer to highly regarded Consultants the world over who are happy to pass on their knowledge. Over the years here, because of word of mouth recommendations, we have attracted and gathered together a patient base of the weird and wonderful, and I mean that in a good way. They are an interesting, loyal and friendly people, who I love working with and I gain great satisfaction when I can help their health, referring on to other experts when necessary. The most difficult and upsetting part of the work is relating to the customer that I have found evidence of a brain tumour, or a leukemia in a child.

Outside of the Practice, I've worked at Whipps Cross Optometry Dept., taught at 3rd Year Clinics, taken in pre-registration students, and sat on numerous committees. But life became fulfilling and improved enormously, especially with the death of my mother which I celebrated. Recently I married Nick, who is a physician, and is the kindest person I know. I've always lived life full on, and I can't imagine slowing down, but I will be very happy to spend more time with him, take time travelling, and catch up on the parts of life I have missed out on.

We recently bought a house together nearby which was literally covered in pink, violet and pale blue paint. Walls, ceilings, light switches, floors, everything. Being an Optometrist, of course I merely speculated that the previous owners had been colour blind. We stripped it all back to the brick, removed partition walls and started again. Then - I found out this house had been a brothel!

Hence the occasional man who knocks at our front door and asks, with a knowing wink, if this is still a hotel!!!! Life is never dull.

E18

Woodford

MENU

CHICKEN	3 00		
6 00	10 00		
		COD	
CHIPS	1 20	2. 40	HADDOCK
SAVELOY		1 10	PLAICE
ROE		2. 20	SCAMPI
PIES		2 20	CALAMARI

LILY WOODS AND HER SON, DAVID WOODS.

WOODS FISH AND CHIP SHOP, 1941 TO 2011. WOODFORD.

Lily's story: I was born in Leyton in 1922, and I met my future husband, John at a Synagogue Youth Club when I was fifteen. He was already working for Larkins, the wet fish shop in Wanstead High Street. By 1941, we had our own wet fish shop in Woodford Bridge, and then we found these premises in George Lane. Trouble was, it was a vandalised bomb damaged site, and used by the local kids as a playground!

The Government rebuilt the premises, we moved in during 1942, and have been serving fish and chips ever since. Initially we were selling wet fish as well. During the war, the shop was rationed, so there was always a queue in the morning for the cod (9d) and bag of chips (4d). When our quota was sold, that was it for the day. Mind you, although John had to stick to buying his ration at the Fish Market, as a twenty year old girl, I seemed to be able to bring home a lot more if I smiled sweetly!

We lived above and behind the shop, but when our customers pushed us into opening a small restaurant, our dining room had to go upstairs as well! Our son, David was born upstairs in 1945, but the shop carried on with John and some staff running it while I was busy elsewhere. David started working here straight from school, then we sent him off to get some more experience with Smith's Fish Shop at the Bakers Arms for a couple of years.

David's story: Just before then, I was sent off on a trawler from Hull for three weeks into the Arctic Circle to experience the conditions and to see how the fish was handled before it came into the shops. What an experience. It was so scary at times I thought I wouldn't ever be coming home! Those guys are tough. When I got home I wrote an article which was published in the trade magazine, Fish Trades Gazette.

One thing that troubled me then, and still does, is the terrible waste of dead fish that get thrown back because it is outside of the quota, or simply the wrong sort of fish. The laws should be changed, so that all kinds of fish can constitute a catch, and not just one species at a time.

So then I came back here and have been at it for forty five years! I make sure that all our fish comes from a well stocked area, and not from a depleted fishing ground. My Dad worked here to his last days, some thirteen years ago, and my Mum is still happily working here, doing the restaurant shopping every day for fresh salad, and bread from over the road at Kistrucks, who are also in this book (p71).

Mum also prepares the books and the VAT for the Accountant, and helps out serving the customers. It keeps her fit and healthy, and I like the fact that she has three cleaners! One for the shop, one for the flat upstairs, and one spare in case of an emergency!

Getting staff to help becomes more and more difficult, but at the moment I enjoy working with Mum serving our regulars who come from as far afield as Wickford, Enfield, Cheshunt and Epping.

Editor's note. Although both Lily and David retired in 2011, the business carries on under new ownership and retains the same name.

CHRIS TOMKINS, MASTER BAKER SINCE 1968.

KISTRUCKS THE BAKERS, SOUTH WOODFORD SINCE 1952.

My great, great, great uncle, surname Henrick Schmeig, was the Pursekeeper to King Wurtenberg in Federal Germany in 1836. That was the last royal connection this family had! His son fled the Schleswig-Holstein war in 1864 and bought his passage to Felixstowe, for the princely price of one cigar! He then herded swine to London to find work, but because one of the pigs died en route, he was sacked, and was housed by the Salvation Army until he qualified and found work....as a baker.

The family has been making bread ever since. However, his bakery (Schmeig) in Stratford was burned down by the anti-German mobs in about 1938, but the irony of that was that he had three sons all fighting in the British army, against the Germans. It was time for a change of name, to Sargent.

My dad bought the Kistrucks bakeries in 1952, with outlets in Chigwell, Woodford Broadway and South Woodford. This one in George Lane used to have twenty six horse drawn carts leaving each morning to supply bread to the East End, up to the very late 1950's. It had previously been Gurney's Bakery back as far as 1926.

So when I was fourteen, I used to cycle to Woodford Green to grease the tins, and forty two years later, I'm still at it! After finishing school locally, I went to the National Bakery School in London for two years, then lived and studied in Bordeaux for fourteen months to gain a greater variety of experience. I gained two Diplomas, but the first one was simply embarrassing. It was a Diploma in 'lavage et leplonge', or washing up!! It was presented to me in front of forty other students and professionals. I'm not sure what the French is for 'wanting to cringe'. My Diplomas hang proudly on the wall to remind myself of my skills!

I've moved up from being 'le lavager et le leplonger', and have been Director of the Bakers Buying Association for over sixteen years, Financial Director of the National Association of Master Bakers and a Trustee of the Bakers Benevolent Society. The Society is based in Bakers Lane, Epping, so named because that was where the inhabitants of the Almshouses at the Bakers Arms, Leyton had to be moved to, many years ago.

I'm pleased to say that all the wheat for our shops grows in Essex, is milled for us in Enfield, and baked on our premises here in Woodford. So it's a true local business, catering for local people. I'm proud of the fact that we don't waste the energy involved in long distance transport, and as a small concern, we create very little of our own waste. We have a good, loyal customer base, which appreciates well made, fresh, wholesome bread, that doesn't simply create steam when being toasted, and then taste of very little!

We have been asked to make some unusual products, the most amusing request being for a certain part of a man's anatomy to be made using pink marzipan, to go inside a chocolate Easter egg, as a gift for his mother-in-law. We politely declined the job, but provided the marzipan instead. We heard later, that the home made version was, shall we say, a bit of a flop!

Retirement seems to be forever on the distant horizon, if not indeed a mirage, but for the present time, I do enjoy being in the position which we hold in the local community.

W.D.CHAPMAN BUTCHERS, WOODFORD GREEN SINCE 1890.

PARTNERS RICHARD AND PETER CHAPMAN AND SISTER, SUE.

The story by Sue: I've traced the family business back three generations to at least 1890. The business has always been in and around Woodford, and we moved to these premises before the 2nd World War. We used to have a slaughterhouse nearby, but because of the regulations around rationing at that time, it had to close, so now we buy in our meat as whole or half carcasses, and butcher it ourselves.

It still comes from the local area, and we make sure it's all free range, so at least we know the animal has had a happy life outdoors. In fact, in the days when carcasses used to hang outside the front of the shop, we could even give our customers the history of the animal, like where it was grazed.

That practice is frowned upon now, as the general public can't cope with the sight of the carcass, I think as a result of the packaging of small pieces of rather anonymous looking meat on supermarket shelves. However in this shop, we are busy with a new generation of customers, who do want to know the origin and care taken with the meat they are buying. It's turning full circle, it seems, but we don't have any plans to hang carcasses outside again!

I came into the business thirty years ago to help out Auntie Ivy, my Dad's sister, who used to be in this cashier's booth. She was very popular as she always gave out Polo mints to customers, but bless her, in later years, she also gave out too much change, so to help protect our profits she retired, and I have been Cashier and Bookkeeper ever since. Away from work, I've always loved horses, and have owned five over the years. In fact, Mick O'Dwyer, the Farrier in this book (p63), looked after my horses hooves for me! I took the horses to local show competition standard, but no more for me, as I ended up on my back in the dirt too many times for my own good! It still hurts me sometimes!

My brother Richard has been here for about fifty years, and Peter has been making all our sausages and burgers by hand for something like forty five years! We have another brother, David, who keeps a few cattle, and helps us with the odd order or two. Unfortunately, none of our children show any desire to keep the business going when we retire.

We've had a few funny experiences over the years, like the elderly lady who didn't pay too much attention to her personal hygiene. It was before the days of aerosol air fresheners, so we used to singe chicken feathers in the shop when she left, to improve the aroma! An ex-army chap still shops here for his 'desert chicken,' otherwise known as corned beef. Not sure which name I prefer!

But the funniest story was when I hadn't been working here for very long. A very elderly man came into the shop and wanted to make a confession! He told us that when he was a young lad, he used to deliver meat for us by bike. Do you remember, those bikes with the big basket on the front. This was in the days when Whitehall Road was a dirt track, so it's going back a long, long time. Anyway, in those days, the meat for delivery wasn't wrapped, and he told us he hit a pothole one day, and all the meat ended up in the dirt. He'd kept it secret for all those years that he picked it all up, washed it in the horse trough, and then delivered it!

I'd like to think we've improved our Health and Hygiene standards since then!

ORFORD SUPPLY CO. LTD., WOODFORD. ESTABLISHED c.1949.

PAT AND BOB GROUT, OWNERS SINCE 1985.

The story by Pat: **Long before I met Bob, and just after the War, my Dad was buying up ex war department engine and vehicle parts, and selling them from the back of a van. After his business partner died, Dad carried on, in a premises in Orford Road, South Woodford, and from then on, the name stuck.**

The business, which became a limited company in 1956, moved to our present premises in Mill Lane. The buildings have a long history. Part of one shop was a blacksmith's, and the cobbles and the drain for the horses are still there. Another part was a cobbler's repair shop, and the workshop at the back used to be a school long ago, and also a small factory where potatoes were peeled!

The company had other premises around Essex, and at one time employed thirty staff. Bob took part time work here, and after his two years National Service in 1956, came back full time. Funnily enough, I didn't meet him, romantically speaking, through the business, but at a local youth centre. Later on we were married, and all the family have worked in the business at one time or another. My dad, who eventually retired in 1985, myself, two brothers, Bob and my sister in law!

Now it's run by Bob and me. We are well known in the car industry, supplying auto electrical parts to local Councils, garages and also Marine engineers for their boats and barges on the Thames. Most of the business used to be assembling batteries in the days before they were 'sealed units', and repairing alternators and starter motors. We now rent out part of the workshop to a mechanic who does the dirty work!

The sulphuric acid for the batteries used to be delivered, 500 gallons at a time, and be stored in a huge tank, which is still here in the roof, but thankfully, nowadays it's empty! There is one note of mystery about the workshop, no ghosts or anything from smithy's or schools, but it's the brown coat which hangs on the hook. No one wears it, no one has ever even touched it as far as we know, and certainly no one knows who it belongs to. But we have worked out that it must have been worn by a little old bloke who used to work here, but he left at least twenty five years ago! It feels wrong to chuck it out, and anyway, it's likely to fall to pieces if we move it!

Outside of work, I regularly play golf at Wanstead Golf Club. I had no intentions of taking up golf, but I realised I wasn't seeing much of Bob when he was out on the golf course, so the old saying 'if you can't beat 'em, join 'em', rang in my ears!!

DAVID BASS, WOODFORD.

SHOPKEEPER, INTERNATIONAL FIREARMS, SINCE 1990.

I was born in Whipps Cross Hospital in 1975, but the first real shock of my life was at fourteen years old. I was at Buckhurst Hill Boys School, and it closed, which meant that all of us boys, wet behind the ears when it came to girls, got transferred to Loughton Girls School! What a result that was, but unfortunately, my education went rapidly downhill while I was distracted. The year we took our exams also coincided with the introduction of the 'new' system called GCSEs, and our teachers couldn't even work out how to teach us, so I flunked my exams. That's my excuse anyway.

I left as soon as I could, aged fifteen, had the weekend off, then went out and got two jobs. One with Iceland, the frozen food company, and the other one here at International Firearms. I was buying some air rifle pellets, saw that a Saturday person was required, and basically fibbed about my age. My height and build helped me kid the owner I was over sixteen.

What was I doing buying pellets at fifteen? Well, when I was twelve, I asked my Dad to buy me a gun, but he refused. So typically, I asked my Mum, and she agreed, but it would have to be kept secret from Dad. She was okay about it as she had been a tomboy in her youth, and went round with boys and airguns. So when my Dad was at work she taught me how to shoot in the back garden! By the time I was fourteen, I enrolled at a local gun club, and fortunately Dad was okay with that, so from then on the secret could be relaxed.

At the club, the Roding Rifle and Pistol Club, where I'm still a member, I was taken under the wing of Janet Raymond, an England International, and flag bearer at the 1978 Commonwealth Games in Canada. My discipline is pistol, but it took me fifteen years to progress sufficiently to finally beat Janet, by which time she was in her 60's! My best result so far, was becoming Essex champion in the 10 metre pistol, and then going on to win the Nationals at Bisley! My business colleague, Karl came second at the same meeting! I was delighted for him, as we had represented the business well.

Going back to when I was seventeen, I was a roadie for a friend's band, and I met Rachel at a gig. We stayed just friends for years, but finally got it together properly to get married ten years ago, and we have one son, James. Recently I asked Rachel to aim and test out a paintball gun at my back, and despite the fact that she shot me in the buttock instead, we are still friends!!

I had left Iceland and was working in an industrial laundry, when I got 'promoted' to manage the night shift, in charge of twenty five people. It was a baptism of fire, but I certainly learned how to run a business. So, while I was still working in the gun shop only one day a week, my boss here offered to sell the business to me as he needed to retire. Rachel and I sold our flat, bought the business, and moved in upstairs for a while. I must admit, I was late for work sometimes and I couldn't even blame the traffic.

One day, the former boss's partner came in with his grandson, who commented that we still had the same dingy colour walls as when the shop opened in 1982! So we redecorated, but kept the original cash till, and stereo! We actually tidied the shop up for the photo, but we usually work in a mess, which is contrary to the advice given in 'the books'. "Start with an immaculate, clear surface" it says, but we know the place backwards, and in fact another gun shop went from being like ours, to clinically tidy, and a year later closed down! I think the customers prefer an old fashioned, messy, slightly careworn place, which presents a friendly feel, rather than stainless steel and glass, which feels a bit cold and clinical.

We have no plans to move away, but instead we intend to invest in new machinery to specialise in the customisation of guns. But we are not investing in a new filing cabinet. This old one has sold many guns, as we use it for target practice, and to show customers how powerful certain guns are!!

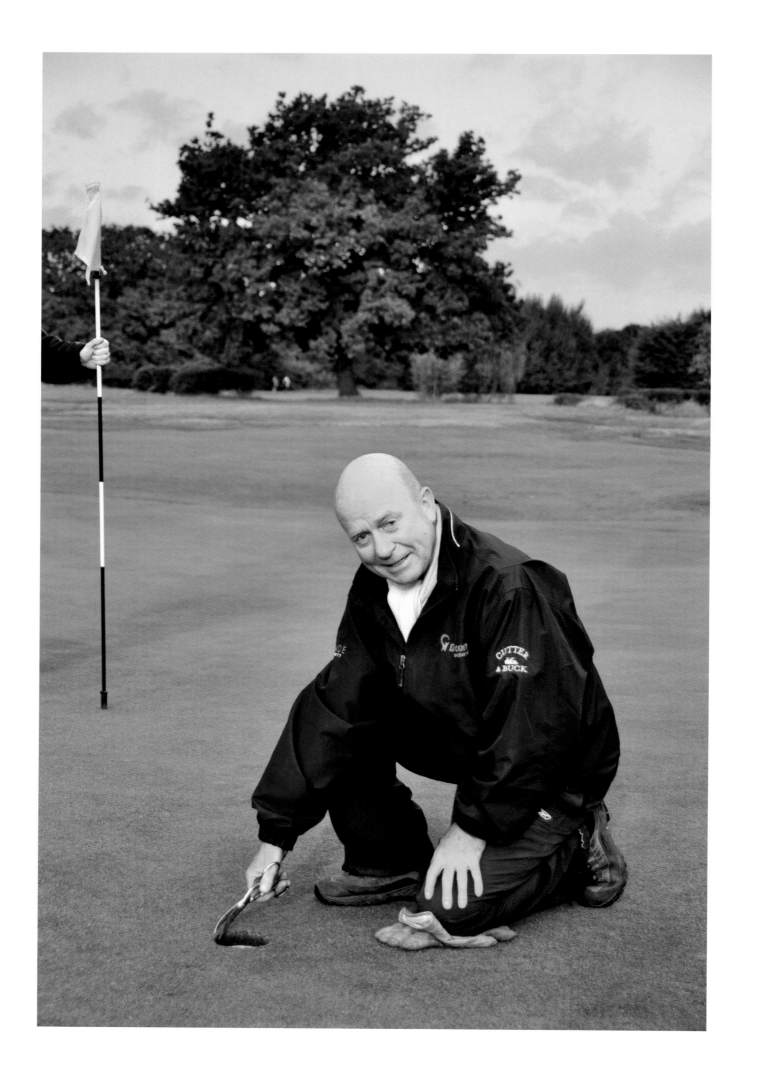

STUART RUNCIMAN, GREENKEEPER SINCE 1970.

RETIRED AS HEAD GREENKEEPER, WOODFORD GOLF COURSE 2013.

I was born in 1948 in a small maternity home opposite Chingford Golf Course, and my classroom at senior school also overlooked the Golf Course! I never imagined I'd end up keeping greens. At school, I especially enjoyed art. In fact, at primary school, I won a competition sponsored by Fry's Chocolates with my painting of the Nativity. I remember really enjoying eating the prize!

But I wanted to be outside, so I left school at sixteen, and found work at Pipers cattle farm in High Beech. We used to take the cattle down to Wanstead Flats by truck, let them graze, then walk, or to use the correct terminology, drive them back to High Beech. When we crossed Woodford Golf Course, again I never imagined I'd be keeping the greens there! Those were the days when 'commoners', who owned land adjoining Epping Forest, were allowed to let their cattle roam free in the Forest area, which of course included the roads around Wanstead, Woodford and up to Epping. The cows certainly slowed the traffic down when they walked along the Epping New Road, but the privilege was removed in 1996 after the Foot and Mouth, and BSE outbreaks.

Back on the farm, I showed my boss some of my art work, and he persuaded my Mum to send me to study art and three years later I gained a Degree in Textile Design. I won a couple of bursaries from the Royal Society of Arts, which enabled me to travel across America and later, Turkey and Persia (Iran). I had fun travelling and seeing different societies, with lots of colour in fabrics, and unfortunately, witnessing the poverty in Turkish fishing villages, which are now popular tourist traps. However, in the States, I picked pears in California to earn some money, and also met the boxer Rocky Marciano, who was a charming man. In fact I travelled with him on the way to the airport, where he caught the plane which crashed, so I was one of the last people to speak with him.

After college I made some money through textile and greeting card design, but at twenty two, I realised that I needed to earn a wage, and the outdoors called again, this time through an advert for an Assistant Greenkeeper at the Woodford Golf Course. Ernie, the Head, taught me until he retired at the age of eighty. As this was in the days before automation, he was very fit, because we walked fourteen miles a day, mowing, pruning, and digging. Ernie lived until his 98th year, and one of my memories of him was when we were clearing ditches. A weasel clamped it's jaws round his boot, and he was hopping around, hollering and trying to shake the animal off, looking like something from a Monty Python sketch!

I still like cattle as they are very gentle animals, but I must admit I got irritated with them when they walked across the course (including Pipers' cows). They are naturally inquisitive, and would come up to a flag on the green, nudge it, then dance around it! It took an age on my hands and knees to dig out the hoofmarks. But I do miss them really.

Ernie used to be a bit brutal with the perimeter of the 34 acre Course, but I'd like to think I've been more creative with the surroundings to make it a pleasant place to play golf. I've been working with my assistant Steve for twenty nine years now, and together we use our experience and expertise to try to keep the greens in perfect condition, resiting the holes regularly, and maintaining the fairways and perimeters. Fortunately I haven't provided him with a laugh by been attacked by weasels! I love the outdoors and the surrounding forest, and it feels more like a hobby rather than a job. Steve (who is holding the flag in the photo), will take over from me this year when I retire from full time work, but I'll carry on a couple of days a week.

I was made an Honorary Member of the Golf Club in their Centenary year in 1990, even though I don't play golf! However, I created caricatures of the Members for the Centenary book, and I plan to get back to some art appreciation in my 'retirement', as well as continuing to enjoy the peace of the forest in this area, where I've always enjoyed living.

CHRYSTALLS THE CHEMIST, WOODFORD BROADWAY c.1904?

VIC IRVINE, CHIEF PHARMACIST SINCE 1988.

I think you know that adventure is in your blood when your Great Grandfather was an American Indian, nicknamed 'Moses', as he was a found orphan, adopted by missionaries in Pennsylvania. As an adult he ducked off a whaling ship in New Zealand and set up home there. So really, I had no family name until I adopted my stepdad's name. I was born in '42 to a Mum from Northampton who travelled and met my Dad in Auckland, New Zealand.

I loved my early years out in Henderson, a country town with a two room school – one room for Primary and the other for Juniors. I used to ride there on horseback, and leave the horse in the school paddock for the day until going home time. We were barefoot most of the time, and I noticed some kids came in with purple feet! They had been helping with the grape pressing at their homes, as the area had been settled by Dalmatian immigrants (modern day Croatia), who brought their wine making skills to establish the very first vineyards in NZ. I still see bottles of wine with some of my old schoolmates' names on them as they are the present day owners of the vineyards.

There was so much exciting stuff to learn at school, and at break times, we would roam the fields, hide in hedges, and climb trees to our hearts' content. Then, when I was ten, our teacher was discussing the pain killer Aspro, and asked us to find out the active ingredient. I went next door to the Primary room, and found an empty box, with the words 'Acetylsalicylic acid'. From that moment, I was hooked on Chemistry, and chemical reactions.

Fortunately, I had a great Chemistry teacher in High School, who fuelled my passion for the subject, and I decided to leave school at sixteen to take an Apprenticeship at a local Pharmacy that would last four years. As apprentices, we would have to soak wheat in arsenic, to be put under the grape vines to kill any birds that dared come along! I'm glad that's no longer practised, partly because we weren't given protective gloves to wear! Other than that, we made up lots of lotions and potions from the raw ingredients, weighed in Grains, or measured in Minims or Drams, from the Doctor's explicit prescription. A far cry from modern pharmaceutical prescriptions.

After a youth of rugby and sailing, I qualified as a Pharmacist, and headed for London in 1964, as I'd heard it was such an exciting place full of amazing women!! I registered with The Pharmaceutical Society and found work in a Pharmacy straightaway – the first of 65 such locum positions I had in my career. After a couple of years, I got bitten by the travel bug – badly, and there wasn't a remedy available on the shelves. I cleaned boilers on a ship across the Pacific through Tahiti to San Francisco, converted an American School bus with friends and drove down to the Mexican Olympics, slept on beaches, took the Trans Siberian Railway to Tokyo, and worked on a ship along the Vietnam coast, where I witnessed the bombardment by the Americans in the late '60's. I worked as a pharmacist wherever I could, as well as labouring on hog farms, ships, and roads. It was a very exciting decade for me.

In between those, and other trips, I kept coming back to the UK, and I then did two things I promised myself I would never do – marry an Australian – and a Pharmacist - but Janice broke my resolve far too easily, and we've been together for forty three years and raised four smashing kids. We lived in Australia, and New Zealand for a while, but we agreed the UK was best, and amusingly, one of our children was conceived in New Zealand, born in Australia, and lives in the UK. The best of all worlds I think.

We started a pharmacy in Shoreditch and made a roof garden where we would have barbeques, rare in the UK at that time. We'd hear neighbours' kids saying "Mummy, Mummy, that chemist is cooking his food on the roof again"! Business in that area was good, but about 30 years ago, we moved to Woodford and bought Chrystalls, which was the name of the original pharmacist. In 2004 we labelled our bottles "100 years on Woodford Broadway", but a very old man came in and disputed it, claiming that as a three year old in 1904, he used to sit on a grassy bank right here, overlooking a pond! But we've definitely passed 100 years now.

In my time as a Pharmacist I've felt very privileged to be able to help folk, and sometimes humbled, as we used to deliver oxygen canisters and morphine to assist people in their last months of life. The practice is becoming more clinical now and not so much to my liking, but I will miss the people, and the satisfaction of knowing I've been able to help them through a tricky period in their lives.

Over the years, I've collected all the memorabilia here, and here it will stay when I sell up, and I hope the future owner will keep the character of the shop. Apart from golf and family, my retirement will take me back to adventures on the waves, but as ever, I'll always come back to the UK.

CHERRY MILLER, WOODFORD GREEN.

VOICE COACH SINCE 1988.

I was born in Snaresbrook at the end of the 2nd World War. My Dad was a gunner in the RAF, and survived 38 missions over Germany. He never talked about his experiences, and wouldn't even let me have a German pen friend! I was an only child, and spent three of my early years with my parents in Portuguese West Africa (Angola), where Dad worked for a firm of importers. Why only three years? Well, I became undernourished, because all I would take was powdered milk drinks!

So, on our return to this country, I discovered the delights of Fairy Cakes, and all was well with the world! I had a chequered education at St.Joseph's Convent. I was a bit naughty, and once got rapped across the knuckles for the offence of poor handwriting. But I liked the Nuns, and somehow managed to gain the privilege of arranging flowers at Church. At Chingford County High, I discovered the joys of the English Language but was too shy to take on any roles in School plays. I really wanted to be involved in Drama somehow so at thirteen years old, my friends and I used to go to see John Geilgud act in theatres in London – leaving our parents at home!!

Being a girl as an only child in those days, your career path was marriage, and money wasn't to be wasted on Further Education, so short hand typing it was. I loathed it for four years, and then got married instead and started a family, which I thoroughly enjoyed. Being at home, guiding and establishing the minds of children felt such a privilege.

Then I got worried I might turn out to be a lady who lunches, so I went back to formal education. I took 'A' Levels and thought I could be a Social Worker at one point, but found a Course in Drama, Poetry and Literature locally. With my cream suit and 80's shoulder pads, I realised that Social Work wasn't really for me. The course tutor became a good friend of the family, so much so that in his last years, we cared for him. But he didn't fully explain that the course was a Teaching Diploma. I had no intentions of teaching, but what wonderful years. I read everything I possibly could, night and day, and immersed myself totally. Which is probably why I passed!

From 1985 I taught Drama in Primary school, and have been immortalised on a tea towel with the childrens' drawings of the teachers. There I am, with my big, long hair, bigger earrings, and beads. At story telling time the children at my feet would stroke the outrageous shoes I chose to wear. They were lovely kids. I was also teaching privately, and eventually after fifteen years, the form filling at State School became too onerous, so I packed it in and just taught from home, which I still do. It used to be mostly adults, wanting to gain confidence for a wedding speech, or a work presentation. Now it's mostly children, especially Asian youngsters, wanting to learn good techniques for school, university or job interviews. It's no wonder they are successful, because they are diligent in all areas of their education. They are also very loyal, and one of my student's mothers is like my own personal Yell.com. I don't need to advertise, or even yell!

I also used to teach Confidence Speech Classes locally, and had a lot of fun at Leyton in the days when Adult Education was free, and attended by some people trying to save on their heating bills at home. "Why this class?", I might ask a new student, and get the response that the Guitar Class was full! There was a high proportion of Caribbean immigrants who wanted to change the way they spoke, to gain acceptance, work, and to be generally understood. So, when the Head of the Local Authority told me not to change people's voices, I upped and left. Mind you, I was ready, as coming home in the late and cold evenings was becoming a bit unappealing.

But I really enjoyed helping people gain confidence with their voice. If you don't like the way you sound, you won't want to express yourself, but all that can change, and over the years I've received some lovely letters from clients, thanking me for helping them deliver good speeches or presentations in public, after starting with me in a nervous sweaty state. There are all sorts of reasons why peoples' speech isn't clear, but one sad case I recall was a man in his forties, who had a real inability to open his mouth enough to speak clearly. As a child, his broken jaw was wired, but when the wires were removed, he was never told that he could now exercise his jaw. So he didn't – ever. I helped him to open his mouth properly for the first time in years!!

Was my finest hour appearing on The Only Way is Essex? I was 'found' and was asked if I could appear on the programme, giving a speech lesson to one of the young characters. I accepted, rather naively, so we had eight film cameras in this room for the whole day. All for about ninety seconds of film. Fame at last..........?

I have no intention of stopping the work that I love, with people that I like, and whose lives I can improve ever so slightly. And I still could have time to be a lady who lunches!

THE WOODFORD & DISTRICT
HORTICULTURAL SOCIETY
H
125
ALL
MEMBERSHIP
CARDS
TO BE
SHOWN

WOODFORD & DISTRICT HORTICULTURAL SOCIETY. EST. c.1945.

JIM MILLER, DEPUTY MANAGER, AND VOLUNTEER SINCE 1987.

I had what was called a 'wartime education' in Clapton, i.e., our school was appropriated by the WW2 Emergency Services Act, and we ran around the streets for the first three months until our school was partially reopened. We had to sit three to a desk and initially attend part time. Several bombs dropped in our road, and a couple didn't explode, so these craters were barricaded off. After a few days, the police got bored with guarding the site, so we used to pretend to be aeroplanes, and throw stones at the unexploded bomb in it's crater as we flew/ran past!! I suppose I'm lucky to still be here, really!

If you attended elementary school in those days, you were required to leave on the first holiday after your 14th birthday so in May 1946 I joined the Post Office as a messenger. After my National Service came another stint in the Post Office then in 1959 I started work for the National Assistance Board, eventually to become the Department of Social Security. I worked in various offices in London, including Stepney, and as part of my work I would meet youngsters who came to London having heard about the 'streets paved with gold'. I would try to convince them to return home, or otherwise find jobs for them where they could 'live in' with the employer. The last resort was to find accommodation for them in hostels. I enjoyed my work and after rising to the post of Manager in 1981, I finally retired in 1989.

Long before that, in 1953, I was on holiday with my mates in Clacton, and met my future wife at a dance at the Blue Lagoon. It was the 'Ladies invitation', and she asked me to dance because I was taller than her! We're still together, and not dancing so much these days, but since our five children have left home, we have been able to enjoy a couple of extended trips abroad. With less mouths to feed, I also gave up my allotment in Chigwell Road. I'd had allotments since the late '50's, which were a big help with a large family. It was hard work, but very rewarding, growing vegetables to put on the family table.

In 1962 I became a member of the Woodford and District Horticultural Society, which had been operating out of the old air raid shelters under Broadmead railway bridge since the end of the Second World War. Behind the little green door is a maze of rooms, full of all the needs of gardeners and allotment holders at a really good price, so I was down there most weeks buying bits and pieces for my plots.

When I was nearing retirement, I applied to help there as a volunteer, under the watchful eye of old Fred, the Manager. He was a huge font of knowledge, and all the volunteers learned a lot from him right up until he died recently, aged ninety eight. I've been a manager there until recently, but am happy to be Deputy now to Dave, who has been with us for years. We have plenty of banter on a Sunday morning when we open to the public, but a lot of hard work goes on behind the scenes. Goods such as seed potatoes, compost, feeds etc., have to be ordered and delivered to the Depot, or sometimes to our homes. We have to bag these into smaller amounts and price them up, but we offer a greater variety than some Garden Centres.

There's been so many characters come through this little green door over the years. Back in the '60's and '70's when this housing estate was allotments, there would be a queue snaking down the road and round the corner, and it would take thirty minutes to get served. We had a little chap with a ruddy face, wearing a flat cap and a leather apron who would check people's membership cards and patrol the queue, shouting "if yer ain't got yer card, yer ain't coming in"!!

On an Open Day recently, a lady came in, and took me to a corner, pointed at the floor, and told me that was where she and her family slept on a bunk during the war!

People think we are the font of all knowledge with regard to horticulture, and we do try to answer all their questions, including one from a lady who was carefully trying to keep a Lily beetle alive, until we could tell her what it was. Not a bug you want in your garden! Sometimes the customers perhaps do know better than us, including a chap who came in one Sunday morning, struck a pose, and declared "If anything's gunna get it this year, it'll be the cabbages"!

It shocks me to think now, that we used to bag up loose DDT, but even more shocking was the Magnesium of Sulphate that we would chip off a block even when it got damp – so we marked it as 'Danger – Explosive – get Fred to bag it up'! About as safe as throwing stones at unexploded bombs!

It's all very safe here nowadays, so I'll enjoy carrying on working behind the little green door for as long as I can.

PHILIP NORMAN, MUSICIAN AND CONDUCTOR SINCE 1965.

WOODFORD SYMPHONY ORCHESTRA. FOUNDED 1963.

I grew up in a house which backed onto West Ham Cemetery and, as I saw grave diggers digging holes in the earth and drinking cups of tea, I thought that this would be an ideal job. Our only toilet was outdoors and I was convinced that if I didn't get back indoors quickly when flushing after dark, something from one of the graves would get me. Three generations plus an aunt and uncle lived in this little house with no bathroom, so to get some peace on a Sunday afternoon, my parents packed me off to Sunday school at St Margaret's, Leytonstone. Here, I went on to join the choir – my practical introduction to music. After piano and then organ lessons, at the age of fifteen, I became organist of Holy Trinity, Harrow Green where I was the (appallingly bad) conductor of the choir!

Whilst a pupil at Leyton County High School for Boys, I decided to follow music studies as a career, rather than maths and physics, despite parental and school opposition. I attended Trinity College of Music in London and emerged with a clutch of their diplomas, and also qualifications from the Royal College of Organists and the Royal College of Music, so I was happy with the direction I was taking.

After teaching music and maths at Campion School in Hornchurch, and some years as Head of Music in Seven Kings High School, I escaped from school teaching to take up a music based job in Norway. Whilst there, I played the organ in churches, conducted choirs and the local orchestra, and was required to compose and arrange music as necessary. This could range from a little choral piece for the opening of a new supermarket, to an arrangement for massed choirs, brass band and organ when Crown Princess Astrid opened a new hospital.

One day, I was asked to give a live interview on radio about what it was like to be an Englishman in Norway at Christmas. Unfortunately, the interviewer had muddled his lists and thought I was the County Chief of Police, so he asked me many questions about how I coped with drunken people during the holiday season. I was baffled, and I expect that the listening public was also baffled by my seemingly off target replies.

On my return to the UK, slap in the middle of the 1991 recession, I was unable to get a job, so I decided to go it alone, earning an income as an organist for weddings, funerals and bar mitzvahs. Alongside this, I used my experiences from Norway to run choral festivals and music workshops. Additionally, I set up a number of online services to facilitate the contact between organists and singers, and people who might want to employ them.

It was at this time that I was discovered by the Woodford Symphony Orchestra who invited me to become their resident conductor. This thirty four strong amateur Orchestra, formed in 1963, performs major Classical works in the Woodford area, holding three main concerts a year. It grows to fifty five in number for some concerts, and calls on professionals if the need arises. At the time of writing, the Orchestra is about to celebrate its 50th anniversary.

The common perception of a conductor is one of an absolute dictator who decides everything about the music. This may be true with the professional orchestras, but at a more amateur level the rehearsing process consists of finding what works well with the orchestra for any particular piece of music. Things are discussed and alternatives tried. But once things are decided, I really take over, and in performance, have to give a strong, unequivocal lead on such matters as tempo, loudness and balance. I have to know the music really well so that, if things drift off course a little bit, I can pull them back into line.

Apart from the regular weekly round of playing in churches for services, weddings and funerals, (which may cover German, Latvian, Norwegian, Danish, Estonian, and Maltese Liturgies) and conducting various choirs and the orchestra, I run a number of larger projects with international outreach. One such is the London Sangerstevne, which is based on the great choral festivals in Norway. Started in 2004, this now attracts choirs from across Europe and the USA, involving up to as many as 1000 singers, with individual choirs performing any style from Barbershop to Baroque – and more. Even though these events can sometimes be quite stressful, I always get a tremendous sense of satisfaction when the choirs mass together for the finale.

It's an interesting lifestyle: the hours are long and irregular, there's no sick pay and no holiday pay. But on the other hand, I am my own master and there's lots of opportunity for innovation and entrepreneurial experimentation.

COLIN BENT, WOODFORD. (INTERVIEWED 2010 - DEC'D 2012).

CLOCK REPAIRER AND RESTORER FROM 1962 TO 2012.
ALBION CLOCKS, WOODFORD.

You could say I'm an atomic baby. My parents decided to get on with having children when the 'A' bombs were dropped on Japan! So I started life with a bang in Plaistow in 1946 but then moved to Woodford and was brought up by my Dad, as my Mum died when I was eleven. I was a latch key kid, staying out as long as possible and getting into all sorts of mischief like hunting rabbits by the River Roding, and making pipe bombs and mortars using firework powder. I always wanted a bigger bang than the last, to rattle the local housing estate windows, which I did once!

Schooling wasn't a high point of my life, and it was decided that it wasn't worth extending my education beyond the age of fifteen as I was regarded as a 'disruptive influence'! So a Youth Employment Officer got me an apprenticeship described as a 'golden opportunity' with Camerer Cuss & Co., clock and watch makers in the West End. I really enjoyed being there, and worked there until I was twenty five, witnessing the design for the digital prototype of the Concorde's 'Black Box', which was to replace the old fashioned wired Flight Recorders.

My big break in business came in 1981 when a customer, who liked my style of work, offered me a partnership with a proviso that I would only work for him, but as he offered me a house and workshop, I could hardly refuse and here I am still. Clocks went for big money in those days. I would go to auctions for him, then restore the clocks at a huge mark up and split the profits. Then I got married to Helen in 1984, and resumed self employment. I called the business Albion Clocks, after the name of a lorry. I had been in the Territorial Army, where I discovered a passion for lorries! I bought a Heavy Artillery Tractor, made by Albion, and it is now kept at Duxford Aerodrome Museum. I used it as transport for my wedding to Helen, and on the occasions of the Queen Mother's 90th and 100th Birthdays I drove it down the M11 to Horse Guards Parade at the maximum speed of 25mph - it took ages!

This workshop has seen some interesting events, with the recording of a soundtrack for an episode of a Harry Potter film, a Cash in the Attic TV Programme, and a piece for Disney Playhouse, with children being filmed with cuckoo clocks.

Sadly, the TV antique shows have been part of a huge drop in the prices of top end antiques, so I concentrate now on restoring the clock workings, and project managing the commissioning and making of cases by skilled cabinet makers.

I still have a Tavern clock that I built from scratch in walnut in 1992, and I applied an ageing technique that unwittingly fooled an expert at an enormous International Fair for new works, in Basle. I witnessed a rather heated discussion in German taking place in front of my clock. One man demanded it's removal, as he was convinced it was an antique, so I showed him the photos of the construction process, and asked him how many he would like! He stormed off, and I found out he was the head of the Antiques Section of the Munich Chamber of Commerce!

So where do I go from here? I've been in the business for nigh on fifty years and lived by my wits. Neither of my sons have any inclination to take it on, so it will die with me.

I am the main carer for my wife who is profoundly disabled with MS, so sadly we can't go out as a family. However, I belong to the Redbridge Ramblers, and enjoy walking with them when I can, and as a treat for my 65th, I intend to walk the Coast to Coast across the North of England which takes two weeks. No clocks ticking or chiming. Just the sound of the wind.

Editor's note. Following Colin's unexpected death last year, I have been unable to contact any members of his family, but I am including his photo and interview as a memorial. I wonder if he walked the Coast to Coast.